NEW MORALITY OR NO MORALITY

NEW MORALITY
OR NO MORALITY

EDITED BY

ROBERT CAMPBELL

THE BRUCE PUBLISHING COMPANY / NEW YORK

Library of Congress Catalog Card Number: 71-101719
Copyright © 1969 The Bruce Publishing Company
Made in the United States of America

CONTENTS

INTRODUCTION

White racism, not poverty or cynicism, is the basic cause of black riots in America. Or are the riots caused by "career agitators and criminal elements" among the black? If you agree with the first, you will love Jackson's article and hate Schuyler's. If you sympathize with the second, you will rejoice at Schuyler's presentation.

"Equating abortion, the elimination of a mass of developing cells, with infanticide, euthanasia, and genocide is offensive and patently false." Readers applauding this statement by Dr. Alan Guttmacher will be annoyed by Eunice Shriver's: "legal reform may add to human anguish and social decay," and infuriated by Mary Calderone's: "abortion is the taking of a life . . . a traumatic experience that may have severe kickbacks later on." But perhaps your reaction is quite the reverse.

"It is to the disciples of Sen. Joe McCarthy, whose crusading paranoia has been transmitted to an entire generation of middle class Americans, that student rebels appear subversive." Or do you find more congenial George Kennan's: "One has sometimes to say 'There goes a perverted and willful and stony-hearted youth by whose destructiveness we are all, in the end, to be damaged and diminished.'"

Billy Graham warns: "The so-called new morality is nothing more than the old immorality brought up-to-date." If this draws a fervent amen from you, your adrenalin will flow at Gordon Clanton's conclusion that non-marital sex can be morally good.

Each of the moral issues treated in this book is similarly presented from opposing points of view, giving the reader a brief and challenging profile of the polarizations the American moral scene has engendered. The articles presented were chosen for their competence in projecting a viewpoint held by many fellow American.

This book had its genesis in the efforts of a university professor to make his classes a lively experience for his students. He found that challenging magazine articles captured student interest and made abstract issues come alive for them. Articles which presented conflicting points of view generated controversy among the students, resulted in livelier class discussions, and heightened interest. The controversy motivated students to re-examine their preconceived ideas and change them, or to justify them in the face of opposition.

In addition to presenting the general reader with a profile of the American moral scene, this book has value as a supplementary text for classes in sociology, religion or moral theology, and ethics. Because of the attempt to present polarization, the reader will find in each section an article with which he strongly disagrees, and probably, strongly dislikes. This reaction, hopefully, will encourage the confrontation and re-evaluation so desirable in the classroom.

The book is divided into considerations of public morality and private morality, with an introductory article to set the stage for each. Abortion is included under public morality because of the present controversy over its public status.

My heartfelt thanks go to Lydia Ryan Galton, trade book editor for Bruce Publishing Company, for her several valuable suggestions which have been incorporated into this book.

Robert Campbell

PUBLIC MORALITY

HAS THIS COUNTRY GONE MAD?

BY DANIEL P. MOYNIHAN

When at length the history of this time comes to be written, it seems certain that one public event will be thought different from all others, and that is the murder of John F. Kennedy. I was in the White House at the moment word arrived that the President was dead. Somehow the scene had been set for just such news. The ebullient, vibrant tone of that building in those days had already vanished. The lights, as I recall, were dimmed. Probably they weren't in fact, but that is the recollection. For certain, a new rug was being laid in the President's oval office, and some of his furniture was stacked in the hallway, as if a change were about to occur. No one was told the President was dead. Rather, of an instant, everyone present knew. The President's men—Sorensen, Dungan, Riordan—stood dazed, apart, alone, knowing what had ended. One

Daniel Moynihan, the former Director of the Joint Center for Urban Studies of the Massachusetts Institute of Technology and Harvard University, is now President Nixon's Assistant for Urban Affairs and Executive Secretary for the Council for Urban Affairs.

"Has This Country Gone Mad?" originally appeared in the Saturday Evening Post *(May 4, 1968) and is reprinted here through the courtesy of the author.*

man only seemed to sense what had begun. Striding to
the telephone on O'Donnell's desk, he picked up the
receiver: "This is Mr. Bundy. Please get me Secretary
McNamara." One's senses awoke. America had entered an age of violence.

Violence has rarely been altogether absent from
American life, and it has ever been part of our fantasies. (And in curiously persisting ways: Union soldiers in the Civil War read dime Western novels between battles, much as marines in Vietnam watch cow-
boy shoot-'em-ups on TV when they can find a moment's peace.) But I think the violence of this age is
different: It is greater, more real, more personal, suf-
fused throughout the society, associated with not one
but a dozen issues and causes. It is invoked by the most
rational, public and respected of our institutions, as
well as by the most obscure and piteous lunatic.

None need search far for the manifestations of
this new age. First of all is the incredible experience
of the Vietnam War, where our Government persists
alone and adamant in a course of destruction. It is as
outwardly convinced of its rationality as the rest of the
nation is, increasingly, of its fundamental immorality,
and the rest of the world of its madness. Sen. Eugene
McCarthy recently stated that, as we continue the incredible devastation dictated by our present policy,
America itself is in danger of becoming an "outcast"
nation in the world. This is the painful truth. Already
a kind of mad logic is making its way back from the
battlefield, as in the words of the immortal American
officer who explained it was necessary to "destroy" a
particular town in order to "save" it.

At home, the rise of black violence has been an
equally ominous and irrational turn. The civil-rights
revolution, once, only months ago, the very embodi-
ment of our pride as a free people and our sense of
mastery over events, has of a sudden become almost

a caricature of just those national tendencies it was directed against. Everywhere, apparently, initiative has passed to leaders whom [former] President Johnson has properly described as vulgar men, half educated in their utterances and wholly sincere only in their destructiveness. The President's Commission on Civil Disorders was justified in its warning that this nation—*this* nation—is moving "toward two societies, one black, one white—separate and unequal." The commission, moreover, had every reason to locate the fundamental sources of this division in white racism. Yet many events of the recent past have given rise to an equally justified feeling on the part of whites that black racism and lawlessness are hastening this division. WHITE CABBY SLAIN AT NEGRO CAMPUS reads a recent headline of an almost routine story on page 68 of *The New York Times*.

And now the violence of the military overseas and in the cities at home has itself induced a reaction of still greater violence. White terrorism against Negroes is an old and hideous aspect of American life, but it was typically the act of slack-jawed, illiterate sadists, or frenzied mobs in the deep South. Now it seems to be becoming a pastime for suburban housewives, taking target practice before television cameras, filling black silhouettes with white holes. Protest against war has been an old and honorable tradition in America, but with this war the peace movement itself has turned violent, threatening elected officials, and taking bodily possession of those who symbolize policies it opposes. And for the people at large, crime in the streets has emerged, precipitously, as one of the single most important political issues of the election year.

One group after another appears to be withdrawing its consent from the understandings and agreements that have made us one of the most stable democracies in the history of the world. Right and Left the conviction of conspiracy mounts. A master symbol of this crisis of confidence is the apparent, ever-widening belief among the citizenry that the assassination of President Kennedy remains unexplained. It is as certain as things are likely ever to be that the Government has told the truth about that event. But it is also certain that it told the truth badly. The effort to reassure the nation that nothing terrible ever really happens to the United States was carried out with such essential casualness that the Warren Commission's *Report* seems to have produced just the opposite of its intended impression on the public.

With this uncertainty in the background, the espousal of violence and violence itself mount on every hand: private crime, organized crime; civil disorder at home to the point of insurrection, violence abroad on a scale unimagined. The sheer effort to hold things together has become the central issue of politics in a nation that began the decade intent on building a society touched with moral grandeur. Increasingly men of the center watch with dismay. Another symbol of the time has emerged: the repeated reference to William Butler Yeat's prophetic poem *The Second Coming:*

> *Things fall apart; the centre cannot hold;*
> *Mere anarchy is loosed upon the world,*
> *The blood-dimmed tide is loosed, and everywhere*
> *The ceremony of innocence is drowned;*
> *The best lack all conviction, while the worst*
> *Are full of passionate intensity.**

A good many Americans—typically they are drawn from our best-educated, most secure, even priv-

* *From "The Second Coming," by W. B. Yeats by permission of Miss Anne Yeats and Mr. Michael Butler Yeats.* © *1924 by The Macmillan Company. Renewed 1952 by Bertha Georgie Yeats.*

ileged classes—do not hesitate to conclude from all this that American society is doomed, and make no effort to conceal their great pleasure at this prospect. The "lust for apocalypse," to use Norman Mailer's term, of the children of the American middle class, is something formidable to behold, especially in the sheer glee with which the Ivy League radicals conclude that however well intentioned the American experiment might have been, it is, after all, over.

Andrew Kopkind, writing in the elitist *New York Review of Books* (complete with a model of a Molotov cocktail on the cover), declares that during the past summer war abroad and revolution at home combined "to murder liberalism in its official robes," and that there were few mourners. On a more primitive level, this is pretty much the message of former Gov. George Wallace of Alabama, who will have millions of Americans voting for him for President next fall. In the meantime, in East Harlem, a school official advises black children to get themselves guns and to practice using them. On silhouettes of suburban housewives, perhaps. Across the river in New Jersey a local mayor advises anyone who henceforth tangles with a cop to be prepared to come off second best. The generals ask for tens of thousands more troops to complete the pacification of South Vietnam. Doubtless there are others in Washington who are arguing that the men will be needed for duty in American cities next summer. The President himself has predicted that there will be violence in the cities next summer and the summer after that.

Increasingly the nation exhibits the qualities of an individual going through a nervous breakdown.

Is there anything to be done? Not a great deal, perhaps. The thought that we have genuine control over events is as much a delusion as the conviction that we are helpless in the face of the inevitable. But the one thing we can and must do is to try to understand our collective strength as a people, and to try to see what is happening to that strength.

The great power of the American nation is not the natural wealth of the continent, nor its physical isolation, nor the invigorating mix of peoples that make up our population, nor the genius of scientific research and business enterprise that have made so much of these assets. *Our strength lies in our capacity to govern ourselves.* Of the 123 members of the United Nations, there are fewer than a dozen that existed in 1914 and have not had their form of government changed by force since that time. We are one of those very fortunate few. More than luck is involved. In nation after nation rent by insurrection, subverted by conspiracy or defeated by enemies, it is not luck that has run out, but judgment—the ability to live with one another; to pick wise rulers; to rule wisely. Having been brilliantly successful at just these things, it is understandable that we give no great thought to them, even at times deny them. But in a time of trouble it is necessary to look to fundamentals.

An Englishman, an expert on guerrilla warfare, put it concisely to a Washington friend about a year ago. The visitor was asked why American efforts to impart the rudiments of orderly government seemed to have so little success in underdeveloped countries. "Elemental," came the reply. "You teach them all your techniques, give them all the machinery and manuals of operation and standards of performance, and the more you do it, the more they become convinced and bitterly resentful of the fact, as they see it, that you are deliberately withholding from them the one all-important secret that you have and they do not, and that is the knowledge of how to trust one another."

That is, to be sure, the secret, and nothing has made it a more open one than the strains that are

now showing in American society because of the withdrawal of trust by so many individuals and groups.
Clearly it is the task of those who are concerned with
the health of the society to preserve the large and still
preponderant trust that remains, and to regain that
trust which has been lost.

The first task is the one bequeathed us by President Eisenhower in his farewell address: To develop
institutional means of controlling the military-industrial
complex which, *through no one's fault,* so easily leads
governments to overestimate the effectiveness of controlled violence—and thereafter the possibility of keeping violence under control.

The war in Vietnam is not, after all, the work of
generals or munitions makers. If anything, it is the result of the strategic and political thought of liberal professors who scarcely understood the forces they were
unleashing for the very reason that those forces were
themselves so neutral and apolitical. But surely a people of the political genius that Americans have shown
over the centuries can find ways to control the potential
for violence of this military-industrial complex which
has come into existence in the past three decades. But
first we must acknowledge that it does exist, and that
it is an institutional problem—not a problem of evil
men, but simply of changed circumstances.

A second and equally urgent task is to impose
effective restraints on black violence at home. It would
no doubt help if everyone, from the President down,
would stop predicting—and thereby legitimating—
such violence, but the decisive restraints will have to
come from within the black community. Social control
in a group, like self-discipline in an individual, is fundamentally an internal affair; external restraints probably impede rather than hasten the development. In
the British Navy it is remarked that the enlisted men
did not begin to discipline themselves until flogging

was abolished, and this is a lesson many white and black leaders of this moment could usefully ponder. The basis for this social control lies in the concept of black power, defined as the control of public offices and resources routinely acquired by any sizable group of citizens using their vote for common objectives. The truly *radical* Negro leaders see this. They have concluded that violence is a disaster to the Negro cause.

If there is one thing we know about property-owning democracies such as ours (or France's or England's) it is that they grow more conservative, not less, in the face of lower-class violence. Random acts of violence, for example, proved a disaster to the American labor movement in the late nineteenth century. A similar fate apparently befell Nat Turner's slave revolt a generation earlier.

But as the most perceptive Negro leaders see, the most serious setback from rioting has to do not with white attitudes but with black ones. Contrary to every white liberal presumption, riots appear to leave black lower-class communities emotionally spent and politically exhausted, useless to those who would truly organize them. Such problems are complex, and answers are elusive, but one thing is clear. What the black community needs now is not excuses for its weaknesses, but encouragement to develop its strengths, and that means above all a turning away from violence.

And the same applies to the educated middle-class youth of the nation, who seem so repelled by the present state of civilization that their prescription is to "start over again." For them, individual and collective violence is so utterly a part of experience that it now is an obsession. ". . . The issue of violence," writes Kenneth Keniston, the psychologist, "is to this generation what the issue of sex was to the Victorian world. . . . The question on which our survival as individuals and as a world depends is: Can we create formulations and forms to control historical and psychological violence before their fusion destroys us all?''

However much (it is after all not very much) the young radicals themselves have resorted to violence, it is clear that the most sensitive and alert of the young people in this nation are now more awake to this issue than any generation in our history—and prepared to make the most awful decisions in terms of the issue. This is perhaps the single most hopeful fact of our national life today. To listen to a young Harvard graduate student discuss the decision he must make, either to be drafted or to leave his country and live the rest of his life in exile, is to understand that this is a generation that may outrage us but has not failed us. To the exclusion of the most precious things, these young people have turned attention to the most important.

And so must we all. The urgent task of liberals and conservatives alike is to decry the descent to violence as a way of life, and to decry most especially any legitimation of it in terms that the failure to enforce this right, or to redress that wrong, somehow makes violence inevitable and therefore acceptable. It is nothing of the sort. The common (and quite possibly groundless) assumption that there will be monstrous rioting this summer is just that—monstrous. Prior to the President's [Johnson, 1968] announcement that he would not run, the apparent determination of some peace groups to prevent him by criminal assault from campaigning among the people this summer was just that—criminal. There must be a stop to this trend toward violence, and in particular, an immediate and passionate objection to any voice that gives aid and comfort to the present drift of events. That is almost a violent statement itself, but one surely warranted in the present state of the American republic.

THE RIOT COMMISSION REPORT— A SUMMARY

BY DONALD JACKSON

"This report isn't for black Americans. They know how it is. It's for white Americans, who don't know."

The speaker was a staff member of the President's National Advisory Commission on Civil Disorders, and the report he referred to is that commission's assessment of a beleaguered society which has failed to live up to its ideals.

The report of the "Riot Commission," issued this week, is in many ways a bold document. Throughout its 250,000 words its message is agonizingly clear: America is and has always been a racist society. Bigotry penetrates every level and every region of the nation—middle class and lower class, North and South, business and labor, education, medicine and journalism. The causes of the riots that occurred in dozens of American cities last summer were not hot-eyed hoodlums bent on destruction nor organized conspiracies directed by a revolutionary force. The causes were ig-

Donald Jackson is an associate editor for Life *magazine, and the author of many articles on political and social issues.*

"The Riot Commission Report" originally appeared in Life *magazine, March 8, 1968,* © *1968 Time Inc., and is reprinted by permission.*

norance, apathy, poverty and, above all, a pervasive discrimination that has thwarted and embittered the American Negro in every avenue of his life.

The commission interviewed more than 130 witnesses, from government officials and policemen to leaders of black militant groups, and employed experts in economics, history, sociology, law enforcement, education and other fields. In a language sometimes dramatic, sometimes angry and sometimes strangling on jargon and statistics, the report pursues every thread the riots left exposed. Included is a chapter describing riots and near riots in eight places (Tampa, Cincinnati, Atlanta, Newark, northern New Jersey, Plainfield, N.J., New Brunswick, N.J., and Detroit); another which catalogues the most frequent grievances of the ghetto dweller and profiles a typical rioter; a historical sketch of the Negro in the United States; analyses of urbanization, the ghetto environment and the relations of police and citizens; and a broad sweep of recommendations touching on employment, education, housing, welfare and law enforcement. Along the way, tucked in amid the endless statistics and the repeated calls for "communication" and "coordination," are dozens of facts and conclusions that illustrate the report's message.

The commission laid waste many of the quick and facile judgments about the riots themselves—their nature, severity and origin:

Invariably, the outbreaks were triggered by "routine arrests of Negroes for minor offenses by white police."

Seventy-four of the 83 dead and 1,185 of the 1,897 injured were civilians, mainly Negroes.

Although the rhetoric of black militants helped foster an atmosphere conducive to rioting, there was no evidence of organization or conspiracy.

Though there were 164 disorders in 128 cities,

only eight were classified as major; most of the rest
were quickly quelled.

"There was widespread . . . exaggeration" of the
presence of snipers. "What is probable, although we
could not secure firm evidence, is that there was at
least some sniping. What is certain is that the amount of
sniping attributed to rioters, by law enforcement offi-
cers as well as the press, was highly exaggerated. . . .
Most reported sniping incidents were demonstrated to
be gunfire by either police or National Guardsmen."

The "typical rioter" was an unmarried Negro male
between 15 and 24, a high school dropout, urban-born,
probably an unskilled laborer employed off and on.

There was a remarkable unanimity on the part of
ghetto residents about their major grievances. The
commission listed them in order of the intensity of
feeling they aroused: 1. Police practices. 2. Unemployment and "underemployment" (part-time or un-
steady jobs). 3. Poor housing. 4. Poor education. 5.
Poor recreation facilities and programs. 6. Ineffective
grievance mechanisms. 7. Disrespectful white attitudes.
8. Discriminatory justice. 9. Inadequate federal programs. 10. Poor municipal services. 11. Discriminatory
commercial and credit practices. 12. Inadequate welfare programs.

The commission asked a sampling of rioters in
Detroit and Newark whether they thought America
was worth fighting for. In Detroit, 39.4% said no. In
Newark, the figure was 52.8%.

Beyond the immediate details of the riots, the
commission also uncovered countless statistics which
cumulatively profile the bleakness and despair of ghetto
life:

The Negro population is growing significantly faster than the white population, and it is younger. The
median age of American Negroes is 21.1, of white 29.1.
One out of nine Americans was black in 1966; by

1972 the proportion will be one out of eight. The great majority of Negroes (70%) live in cities, to which they have migrated in the last 50 years from the rural South. The white population, meanwhile, has steadily moved to the suburbs, which are 96% white.

Negroes with the same education and the same jobs as whites are paid less. For the same size housing units, Negroes pay an average 10% higher rent.

More than 2.3 million Negro children under 15 are living in circumstances below the poverty level ($3,335 a year for a family of four).

"Young people in the ghetto are acutely conscious of a system which appears to offer rewards to those who illegally exploit others (narcotics sellers, numbers runners, etc.) and failure to those who struggle under the traditional responsibilities. . . . Many adopt exploitation and 'hustling' as a way of life . . . and this pattern reinforces itself from one generation to the next."

Black mothers die in childbirth four times as often as white mothers do; black babies die in infancy three times as often as white babies. A Negro's life expectancy is 64.1 years, a white's 71 years.

Few chain stores operate in the ghettos and few ghetto residents own automobiles. As a result they shop at small stores where prices are generally higher and quality is often lower.

Negroes have been unable to follow the tracks of earlier ethnic minorities out of the slums into the suburbs, partially because the whole economy has changed —with fewer demands today for unskilled labor—but primarily because of discrimination in housing and labor unions.

A survey in one city found that it took police four times as long to respond to a call from a Negro area as compared to a call from a white area of the city.

There is one Negro on the 1,502-man Michigan

state police force; in New Jersey, there are five Negroes on a force of 1,224. Phoenix has seven Negro policemen on a 707-man force, Boston 49 out of 2,504.

Thirty-seven percent of adult American Negroes are "functionally illiterate."

Through the dogged accumulation of such facts the commission reached its central conclusion: in the words of its chairman, Illinois Governor Otto Kerner, it is that "racism, not poverty or cynicism," was the basic cause of the riots and of the current schism in American life. As a commission staff member put it, "We've got to see it as a system and attack it as a system."

The "system," of course, has existed in America since the beginning. The Declaration of Independence says "all men are created equal," but the commission records the persistent violation of that ideal—Negro witnesses in Southern courts swearing on separate Bibles and Negro corpses buried in separate cemeteries, destitute Negroes excluded from "soup kitchen" lines during the Depression, separate blood banks for white and black soldiers during World War II, brutal repression of Negro voters down to the present day, and thousands of unpunished murders and lynchings.

The report criticizes policemen for failing to understand or deal with the problems of ghetto residents and the press for not communicating "a sense of the degradation, misery and hopelessness of living in the ghetto." Too often, the report says, "the press acts and talks about Negroes as if Negroes do not read the newspapers or watch TV, give birth, marry, die and go to PTA meetings."

The commission's major recommendations are for the most part familiar. But if they were all adopted they would add up to a true revolution in the government's commitment to Negro equality:

A "national comprehensive and enforceable open-occupancy law," applying to all housing, including single-family units.

Movement toward the "development of a national system of income supplementation to provide a basic floor of economic and social security" for all Americans.

An employment goal of one million new jobs in the public sector in the next three years, and an additional million in private industry, aided by government contracts or tax incentives for employers.

Six million new housing units within five years, 600,000 to be built in the first year.

Elimination of the "man-in-the-house" welfare rule and scrapping of the one-year residency requirement for welfare recipients.

Better teachers in ghetto schools, better-trained and more compassionate policemen on ghetto streets.

Future federal education aid to be limited to schools achieving a fixed level of integration.

"Neighborhood city halls" to give ghetto residents a place to get a sympathetic hearing for their problems.

A national gun-control law.

Expansion of the Head Start program to younger children.

The extension and expansion of most existing programs aimed at combating poverty and ghetto conditions and promoting integration.

The bulk of the projected financial burden, predictably, lands on the federal government, but the commission estimates the American bounty as great enough to underwrite "an important start on reducing the social deficit in spite of a war and current budget requirements."

But if the report's prescription is familiar, its major thrust is not. What it accomplishes, ultimately, is the destruction of a litany of comfortable assumptions long held by white Americans: that bigotry is an exclusively Southern infection; that Negroes have been held down by poverty, not racism; that hard work and good luck will bring success for anyone; that some "outside force" is responsible for urban uprisings; that Negroes have the same opportunities as other American minorities. Most basic of all, the report questions the assumption that we are fundamentally a decent and humane people. It does not abandon hope, but neither does it offer much evidence for hope. And, in the end, for all the commission's documentation of prejudices and strategies to better the Negro's life, its report is essentially a plea to white America. Here's how it is, the report says, now it's up to you to do something about it. If the choice is to continue the present course, the commission warns that "an 'urban apartheid' with semi-martial law" could result and that, indeed, "we are well on the way to becoming such a divided nation."

THE WRONG WAY
TO FIND JOBS
FOR NEGROES

BY DAVID WELLMAN

In the summer of 1966 I studied a Federal government program designed to help lower-class youths find jobs. The program was known as TIDE. It was run by the California Department of Employment, and classes were held five days a week in the Youth Opportunities Center of West Oakland.

The TIDE program was anything but a success. "I guess these kids just don't want jobs," one of the teacher-counselors told me. "The clothes they wear are loud. They won't talk decent English. They're boisterous. And they constantly fool around. They refuse to take the program seriously."

David Wellman is on the editorial staff of The Movement, *a news journal affiliated with the Student Non-Violent Co-ordinating Committee and Students for a Democratic Society. He is a graduate student in sociology at the University of California at Berkeley and is research coordinator for a study on racism, manhood, and culture in American society.*

"The Wrong Way to Find Jobs for Negroes" is reprinted from Trans-Action *magazine. Copyright © 1968 by Washington University, St. Louis, Mo. by permission of author and publisher.*

"But isn't there a job shortage in Oakland?" I asked. "Does it really *matter* how the kids act?"

"There's plenty of jobs. They're just not interested."

The students were 25 young men and 25 young women selected by poverty-program workers in the Bay Area. Their ages ranged from 16 to 22, and most were Negroes. The government paid them $5 a day to participate. Men and women usually met separately. I sat in on the men's classes.

The young men who took part in TIDE had a distinctive style. They were "cool." Their hair was "processed." All sported sunglasses—very lightly tinted, with small frames. They called them "pimp's glasses." Their clothes, while usually inexpensive, were loud and ingeniously altered to express style and individuality. They spoke in a "hip" vernacular. Their vocabularies were small but very expressive. These young men, as part of the "cool world" of the ghetto, represent a distinctively black working-class culture.

To most liberals these young men are "culturally deprived" or "social dropouts." Most had flunked or been kicked out of school. Few had any intention of getting a high-school degree. They seemed uninterested in "making it." They had long and serious arrest and prison records. They were skeptical and critical of both the TIDE program and white society in general.

The TIDE workers were liberals. They assumed that if the young men would only act a little less "cool" and learn to smooth over some of their encounters with white authorities, they too could become full-fledged, working members of society. The aim of TIDE was not to train them for jobs, but to train them how to *apply* for jobs—how to take tests, how to make a good impression during a job interview, how to speak well, how to fill out an application form properly. They would play games, like dominoes, to ease the pain asso-

ciated with numbers and arithmetic; they would conduct mock interviews, take mock tests, meet with management representatives, and tour places where jobs
might be available. They were told to consider the TIDE
program itself as a job—to be at the Youth Opportunities Center office on time, dressed as if they were at
work. If they were late or made trouble, they would be
docked. But if they took the program seriously and
did well, they were told, they stood a pretty good
chance of getting a job at the end of four weeks. The
unexpressed aim of TIDE, then, was to prepare Negro
youngsters for white society. The government would
serve as an employment agency for white, private enterprise.

The program aimed to change the youngsters by
making them more acceptable to employers. Their
grammar and pronunciation were constantly corrected.
They were indirectly told that, in order to get a job,
their appearance would have to be altered: For example, "Don't you think you could shine your shoes?"
Promptness, a virtue few of the youngsters possessed,
was lauded. The penalty for tardiness was being put
on a clean-up committee, or being docked.

For the TIDE workers, the program was a four-
week exercise in futility. They felt they weren't asking
very much of the youngsters—just that they learn to
make a good impression on white society. And yet the
young men were uncooperative. The only conclusion
the TIDE workers could arrive at was: "They just don't
want jobs."

Yet most of the youngsters took *actual* job possibilities very seriously. Every day they would pump the
Youth Opportunities Center staff about job openings.
When told there was a job at such-and-such a factory
and that a particular test was required, the young men
studied hard and applied for the job in earnest. The
TIDE program *itself*, however, seemed to be viewed as

only distantly related to getting a job. The youngsters
wanted jobs, but to them their inability to take tests
and fill out forms was *not* the problem. Instead, they
talked about the shortage of jobs available to people
without skills.

Their desire for work was not the problem. The
real problem was what the program demanded of the
young men. It asked that they change their manner of
speech and dress, that they ignore their lack of skills
and society's lack of jobs, and that they act as if their
arrest records were of no consequence in obtaining a
job. It asked, most important, that they pretend *they*,
and not society, bore the responsibility for their being
unemployed. TIDE didn't demand much of the men:
Only that they become white.

Putting on the program

What took place during the four-week program
was a daily struggle between white, middle-class ideals
of conduct and behavior and the mores and folkways
of the black community. The men handled TIDE the
way the black community in America has always
treated white threats to Negro self-respect. They used
subtle forms of subversion and deception. Historians
and sociologists have pointed to slave subversion, to the
content and ritual of Negro spirituals, and to the blues
as forms of covert black resistance to white mores.

Today, "putting someone on," "putting the hype
on someone," or "running a game on a cat" seem to be
important devices used by Negroes to maintain their
integrity. "Putting someone on," which is used as much
with black people as with whites, allows a person to
maintain his integrity in a hostile or threatening situation. To put someone on is to publicly lead him to believe that you are going along with what he has to offer
or say, while privately rejecting the offer and subtly

subverting it. The tactic fails if the other person recognizes what is happening. For one aim of putting someone on is to take pride in feeling that you have put something over on him, often at his expense. (Putting someone on differs from "putting someone down," which means active defiance and public confrontation.)

TIDE was evidently interpreted by the men as a threat to their self-respect, and this was the way they responded to it. Sometimes TIDE was put on. Sometimes it was put down. It was taken seriously only when it met the men's own needs.

There was almost no open hostility toward those in charge of TIDE, but two things quickly led me to believe that if the men accepted the program, they did so only on their own terms.

First, all of them appeared to have a "tuning-out" mechanism. They just didn't hear certain things. One young man was a constant joker and talked incessantly, even if someone else was speaking or if the group was supposed to be working. When told to knock it off, he never heard the command. Yet when he was interested in a program, he could hear perfectly.

Tuning-out was often a collective phenomenon. For instance, there was a radio in the room where the youngsters worked, and they would play it during lunch and coffee breaks. When the instructor would enter and tell them to begin work, they would continue listening and dancing to the music as if there were no one else in the room. When *they* were finished listening, the radio went off and the session began. The youngsters were going along with the program—in a way. They weren't challenging it. But they were undermining its effectiveness.

A second way in which the young men undermined the program was by playing dumb. Much of the program consisted of teaching the youngsters how to fill out employment applications. They were given lengthy lectures on the importance of neatness and lettering. After having filled out such forms a number of times, however, some students suddenly didn't know their mother's name, the school they last attended, or their telephone number.

This "stupidity" was sometimes duplicated during the mock job interviews. Five or more of the students would interview their fellow trainees for an imaginary job. These interviewers usually took their job seriously. But after it became apparent that the interview was a game, many of the interviewees suddenly became incredibly incompetent. They didn't have social-security numbers, they couldn't remember their last job, they didn't know what school they went to, they didn't know if they really wanted the job—to the absolute frustration of interviewers and instructors alike. Interestingly enough, when an instructor told them one morning that *this* time those who did well on the interview would actually be sent out on a real job interview with a real firm, the stupid and incompetent were suddenly transformed into model job applicants.

The same thing happened when the youngsters were given job-preference tests, intelligence tests, aptitude tests, and tests for driver's licenses. The first few times the youngsters took these tests, most worked hard to master them. But after they had gotten the knack, and still found themselves without jobs and taking the same tests, their response changed. Some of them no longer knew how to do the test. Others found it necessary to cheat by looking over someone's shoulder. Still others flunked tests they had passed the day before. Yet when they were informed of actual job possibilities at the naval ship yard or with the post office, they insisted on giving and taking the tests themselves. In one instance, some of them read up on which tests were relevant for a particular job, then practiced that test for a couple of hours by themselves.

Tuning-out and playing stupid were only two of the many ways the TIDE program was "put-on." Still another way: Insisting on work "breaks." The young men "employed" by TIDE were well-acquainted with this ritual, and demanded that it be included as part of their job. Since they had been given a voice in deciding the content of the program, they insisted that breaks become part of their daily routine. And no matter what the activity, or who was addressing them, the young men religiously adhered to the breaks.

The program started at 9:30 A.M. The youngsters decided that their first break would be for coffee at 10:30. This break was to last until 11. And while work was never allowed to proceed a minute past 10:30, it was usually 11:15 or so before the young men actually got back to work. Lunch began exactly at 12. Theoretically, work resumed at 1. This usually meant 1:15, since they had to listen to "one more song" on the radio. The next break was to last from 2:30 to 3. However, because they were finished at 3:30 and because it took another 10 minutes to get them back to work, the fellows could often talk their way out of the remaining half hour. Considering they were being paid $5 a day for five hours' work, of which almost half were regularly devoted to breaks, they didn't have a bad hustle.

Trips and games

Games were another part of the TIDE program subverted by the put-on. Early in the program an instructor told the students that it might be helpful if they mastered arithmetic and language by playing games— dominoes, Scrabble, and various card games. The students considered this a fine idea. But what their instructor had intended for a pastime during the breaks, involving at most an hour a day, they rapidly turned into a major part of the instruction. They set aside 45 minutes in the morning and 45 minutes in the afternoon for games. But they participated in these games during their breaks as well, so that the games soon became a stumbling block to getting sessions back in order after breaks. When the instructor would say, "Okay, let's get back to work," the men would sometimes reply, "But we're already working on our math—we're playing dominoes, and you said that would help us with our math."

To familiarize the students with the kinds of jobs potentially available, the TIDE instructors took them on excursions to various work situations. These excursions were another opportunity for a put-on. It hardly seemed to matter what kind of company they visited so long as the visit took all day. On a trip to the Oakland Supply Naval Station, the men spent most of their time putting the make on a cute young WAVE who was their guide. One thing this tour did produce, however, was a great deal of discussion about the war in Vietnam. Almost none of the men wanted to serve in the armed forces. Through the bus windows some of them would yell at passing sailors: "Vietnam, baby!" or "Have a good time in Vietnam, man!"

The men would agree to half-day trips only if there was no alternative, or if the company would give away samples. Although they knew that the Coca-Cola Company was not hiring, they wanted to go anyway, for the free Cokes. They also wanted to go to many candy and cookie factories. Yet they turned down a trip to a local steel mill that they knew was hiring. TIDE, after all, was not designed to get them an interview—its purpose was to show them what sorts of jobs might be available. Given the circumstances, they reasoned, why not see what was *enjoyable* as well?

When the men were not putting-on the TIDE program and staff, they might be putting them down. When someone is put-down, he knows it. The tactic's success *depends* on his knowing it, whereas a put-on is successful only when its victim is unaware of it.

The interview technique

Among the fiercest put-downs I witnessed were those aimed at jobs the students were learning to apply for. These jobs were usually for unskilled labor: post-office, assembly-line, warehouse, and longshore workers, truck drivers, chauffeurs, janitors, bus boys, and so on.

The reaction of most of the students was best expressed by a question I heard one young man ask an instructor: "How about some tests for I.B.M.?" The room broke into an uproar of hysterical laughter. The instructor's response was typically bureaucratic, yet disarming: "Say, that's a good suggestion. Why don't you put it in the suggestion box?" The students didn't seem able to cope with that retort, so things got back to normal.

Actual employers, usually those representing companies that hired people only for unskilled labor, came to TIDE to demonstrate to the men what a good interview would be like. They did *not* come to interview men for real jobs. It was sort of a helpful-hints-for-successful-interviews session. Usually one of the more socially mobile youths was chosen to play the role of job applicant. The entire interview situation was played through. Some employers even went so far as to have the "applicant" go outside and knock on the door to begin the interview. The students thought this was both odd and funny, and one said to the employer: "Man, you've already *seen* the cat. How come you making him walk out and then walk back in?"

With a look of incredulity, the employer replied: "But that's how you get a job. You have to sell yourself from the moment you walk in that door."

The employer put on a real act, beginning the interview with the usual small talk.

"I see from your application that you played football in high school."

"Yeah."

"Did you like it?"

"Yeah."

"Football really makes men and teaches you teamwork."

"Yeah."

At this point, the men got impatient: "Man, the cat's here to get a job, not talk about football!"

A wisecracker chimed in: "Maybe he's interviewing for a job with the Oakland Raiders."

Usually the employer got the point. He would then ask about the "applicant's" job experience, draft status, school record, interests, skills, and so on. The young man being interviewed usually took the questions seriously and answered frankly. But after a while, the rest of the group would tire of the game and (unrecognized, from the floor) begin to ask about the specifics of a real job:

"Say man, how much does this job pay?"

"What kind of experience do you need?"

"What if you got a record?"

It didn't take long to completely rattle an interviewer. The instructor might intervene and tell the students that the gentleman was there to help them, but this would stifle revolt for only a short while. During one interview, several of the fellows began loudly playing dominoes. That got the response they were looking for.

"Look!" shouted the employer. "If you're not interested in learning how to sell yourself, why don't you just leave the room so that others who are interested can benefit from this?''

"Oh no!'' responded the ringleaders. "We work here. If you don't dig us, then *you* leave!''

Not much later, he did.

Sometimes during these mock interviews, the very nature of the work being considered was put-down. During one mock interview for a truck-driving job, some of the men asked the employer about openings for salesmen. Others asked him about executive positions. At one point the employer himself was asked point-blank how much he was paid, and what his experience was. They had turned the tables and were enjoying the opportunity to interview the interviewer. Regardless of a potential employer's status, the young men treated him as they would their peers. On one tour of a factory, the students were escorted by the vice-president in charge of hiring. To the TIDE participants, he was just another guide. After he had informed the students of the large number of unskilled positions available, they asked him if he would hire some of them, on the spot. He replied that this was just a tour and that he was in no position to hire anyone immediately. One youth looked at him and said: "Then you're just wasting our time, aren't you?''

Although shaken, the executive persisted. Throughout his talk, however, he innocently referred to his audience as "boys,'' which obviously bothered the students. Finally one of the more articulate men spoke up firmly: "We are young *men*, not boys!''

The vice-president blushed and apologized. He made a brave attempt to avoid repeating the phrase. But habit was victorious, and the word slipped in again and again. Each time he said "you boys'' he was corrected, loudly, and with increasing hostility.

The students treated State Assemblyman Byron Rumford, a Negro, the same way. The meeting with

Rumford was an opportunity for them to speak with an elected official about the job situation in the state. The meeting was also meant to air differences and to propose solutions. At the time, in fact, the men were quite angry about their rate of pay at TIDE. An instructor had suggested that they take the matter up with Rumford.

The meeting was attended by both the young men and women in the TIDE program. The young women were very well-dressed and well-groomed. Their clothes were not expensive, but were well cared for and in "good taste." Their hair was done in high-fashion styles. They looked, in short, like aspiring career women. The young men wore their usual dungarees or tight trousers, brightly colored shirts and sweaters, pointed shoes, and sunglasses.

The women sat quietly and listened politely. The men spoke loudly whenever they felt like it, and constantly talked among themselves.

Rumford, instead of speaking about the job situation in the Bay Area, chose to talk about his own career. It was a Negro Horatio Alger story. The moral was that if you work hard, you too can put yourself through college, become a successful druggist, then run for public office.

The moment Rumford finished speaking and asked for questions, one of the men jumped up and asked, "Hey man, how do we get a raise?" A male chorus of "Yeah!" followed. Before Rumford could complete a garbled answer (something like, "Well, I don't really know much about the procedures of a federally sponsored program"), the battle of the sexes had been joined. The women scolded the men for their "disrespectful behavior" toward an elected official. One said: "Here he is trying to help us and you-all acting a fool. You talking and laughing and carrying on while he talking, and then when he finishes you want to know about a raise. Damn!''

''Shit,'' was a male response. ''You don't know what you talking about. We got a *right* to ask the cat about a raise. We elected him.''

''We supposed to be talking about jobs,'' said another. ''And we're talking about *our* job. If y'all like the pay, that's your business. We want more!''

The debate was heated. Neither group paid any attention to Rumford, who wisely slipped out of the room.

Battle of sexes—or class conflict?

During the exchanges it became clear to me that the differences in clothing and style between the sexes reflected their different orientations toward the dominant society and its values. In the minds of the young women, respect and respectability seemed paramount. At one point, a young woman said to the men, ''You acting just like a bunch of *niggers.*'' She seemed to identify herself as a Negro, not as a ''nigger.'' For the men, on the other hand, becoming a Negro (as opposed to a ''nigger'') meant giving up much that they considered positive. As one young man said in answer to the above, ''You just ain't got no soul, bitch.''

The women's identification with the values of white society became even clearer when the debate moved from what constituted respect and respectability to a direct attack on a personal level: ''Do you all expect to get a job looking the way you do?'' ''Shit, I wouldn't wear clothes like that if I was on welfare.''

The direction of the female attack corresponded closely with the basic assumptions of the TIDE program: People are without jobs because of themselves. This barrage hit the young men pretty hard. Their response was typical of any outraged male whose manhood has been threatened. In fact, when one young woman gibed, "You ain't no kinda man," some of the fellows had to be physically restrained from hitting her.

One of the men explained that "maybe the reason cats dress the way they do is because they can't afford anything else. Did you ever think of that?"

The woman's response was one I had not heard since the third or fourth grade: "Well, it doesn't matter what you wear as long as it's clean, pressed, and tucked-in. But hell, you guys don't even shine your shoes."

The battle of the sexes in the black community seems to be almost a class conflict. Many observers have noted that the black woman succeeds more readily in school than the black man. Women are also favored by parents, especially mothers. Moreover, the black woman has been for some time the most stable force and the major breadwinner of the Negro family. All these things put Negro women in harmony with the major values attached to work and success in our society. Black men, however, have been estranged from society, and a culture has developed around this estrangement—a male Negro culture often antagonistic to the dominant white society. The black woman stands in much the same relation to black men as white society does.

Even including Rumford, no group of officials was put down quite so hard as the Oakland police. Police brutality was constantly on the youngsters' minds. A day didn't pass without at least one being absent because he was in jail, or one coming in with a story about mistreatment by the police. A meeting was arranged with a sergeant from the Community Relations Bureau of the Oakland police. The students seemed excited about meeting the officer on their own turf and with the protection provided by the program.

In anticipation of his arrival, the fellows rearranged the room, placing all the separate tables together. Then they sat down in a group at one end of the table, waiting for the officer.

Putting down the police

Sergeant McCormack was an older man. And while obviously a cop, he could also pass for a middle-aged businessman or a young grandfather.

"Hi boys," he said as he sat down. His first mistake. He began with the five-minute speech he must give to every community group. The talk was factual, uninteresting, and noncontroversial: how the department is run, what the qualifications for policemen are, and how difficult it is for police to do their work and still please everyone. His talk was greeted with complete silence.

"I understand you have some questions," McCormack finally said.

"What about police brutality?" asked one man.

"What is your definition of police brutality?" the sergeant countered.

"How long you been a cop?" someone shouted.

"Over 20 years."

"And you got the nerve to come on sounding like you don't know what we talking about. Don't be jiving us. Shit, if you've been a cop *that* long, you *got* to know what we talking about."

"Righteous on that, brother!" someone chimed in.

"Well, I've been around a while, all right, but I've never seen any brutality. But what about it?"

"What *about* it?" There was a tone of disbelief mixed with anger in the young man's voice. "Shit man, we want to know why you cats always kicking other cats' asses."

The officer tried to draw a distinction between

necessary and unnecessary police violence. The fellows
weren't buying that. They claimed the police system-
atically beat the hell out of them for no reason. The
officer asked for examples and the fellows obliged with
long, involved, and detailed personal experiences with
the Oakland Police Department. The sergeant listened
patiently, periodically interrupting to check details and
inconsistencies. He tried to offer a police interpretation
of the incident. But the fellows were simply not in a
mood to listen. In desperation the sergeant finally said,
"Don't you want to hear *our* side of the story?"

"Hell no, motherfucker, we *see* your side of the
story every night on 14th Street."

One young man stood up, his back to the officer,
and addressed his contemporaries: "We *tired* of talking! We want some action! There's a new generation
now. We ain't like the old folks who took all this shit
off the cops." He turned to the sergeant and said, "You
take that back to your goddamn Chief Preston and tell
him."

McCormack had a silly smile on his face.

Another youngster jumped up and hollered, "You
all ain't going to be smiling when we put dynamite in
your police station!"

The officer said simply, "You guys don't want to
talk."

"You see," someone yelled, "the cat's trying to be
slick, trying to run a game on us. First he comes in
here all nice-talking, all that shit about how they run
the police and the police is to protect us. And then
when we tell him how they treat us he wants to say we
don't want to talk. Shit! We want to talk, he don't
want to listen."

From this point on, they ran over him mercilessly.
I, with all my biases against the police, could not help
feeling compassion for the sergeant. If the police are
an authority figure in the black community, then this

episode must be viewed as a revolt against authority—
all authority. There was nothing about the man's life,
both private and public, that wasn't attacked.

"How much money you get paid?"

"About $12,000 a year."

"For being a cop? Wow!"

"What do you do?"

"I work in the Community Relations Department."

"Naw, stupid, what *kind* of work?"

"I answer the telephone, speak to groups, and try
to see if the police treat the citizens wrong."

"Shit, we could do that and we don't even have a
high school education. Is that all you do? And get that
much money for it?"

"Where do you live?"

"I'll bet he lives up in the hills."

"I live in the east side of Oakland. And I want
you to know that my next-door neighbor is a colored
man. I've got nothing against colored people."

"You got any kids?"

"Yeah, two boys and a girl."

"Shit, bet they all went to college and got good
jobs. Any of your kids been in trouble?"

"No, not really."

"What do they do?"

"My oldest boy is a fighter pilot in Vietnam."

"What the hell is he doing over there? That's
pretty stupid."

"Yeah man, what are we fighting in Vietnam for?
Is that your way of getting rid of us?"

"Well, the government says we have to be there
and it's the duty of every citizen to do what his country
tells him to do."

"We don't want to hear all that old bullshit, man."

"Hey, how come you wear such funny clothes?
You even look like a goddam cop."

"Yeah baby, and he smells like one too!"

The barrage continued for almost half an hour. The instructor finally called a halt: "Sergeant McCormack has to get back, fellows. Is there anything specific that you'd like to ask him?"

"Yeah. How come Chief Preston ain't here? He's always talking to other people all over the country about how good the Oakland cops are and how there ain't going to be no riot here. Why don't he come and tell us that? We want to talk with the chief."

The next day, Deputy Chief Gain came—accompanied by the captain of the Youth Division, the lieutenant of that division, and a Negro sergeant. It was a formidable display of police authority. The youngsters were noticeably taken aback.

Chief Gain is a no-nonsense, businesslike cop. He takes no static from anyone, vigorously defends what he thinks is correct, and makes no apologies for what he considers incorrect. He is an honest man in the sense that he makes no attempt to cover up or smooth over unpleasant things. He immediately got down to business: "All right now, I understand you guys have some beefs with the department. What's the story?"

The fellows started right in talking about the ways they had been mistreated by the police. The chief began asking specific questions: where it happened, when it happened, what the officer looked like, and so on. He never denied the existence of brutality. That almost seemed to be assumed. He did want details, however. He always asked whether the youth had filed a complaint with the department. The response was always No. He then lectured them about the need to file such complaints if the situation was to be changed.

He explained the situation as he saw it: "Look fellows, we run a police force of 654 men. Most of them are good men, but there's bound to be a few rotten apples in the basket. I know that there's a couple of men who mistreat people, but it's only a few and we're trying our best to change that."

"Shit, I know of a case where a cop killed a cat and now he's back on the beat."

"Now wait a minute—"

"No more waiting a minute!" someone interrupted. "You had two cops got caught taking bribes. One was black and the other Caucasian. The black cat was kicked off the force and the white cat is back on."

"Yeah, and what about that cat who killed somebody off-duty, what about him?"

"Hold on," Gain said firmly. "Let's take these things one at a time." He didn't get very far before he was back to the "few rotten apples" argument.

"If it's only a few cops, how come it happens all the time?"

The deputy chief told them that he thought it was the same few cops who were causing all the problems. "Unless you file complaints each time you feel you've been mistreated, we can't do anything about it. So it's up to you as much as it is up to us."

For the first time in weeks, I intruded into the discussion. I pointed out to Gain that he was asking citizens to police their own police force. He had argued that in most situations the department had a good deal of control over its own men—the same argument the police had used against a civilian-review board. Now he was saying the opposite: that it was up to the citizens. This seemed to break the impasse, and the students howled with delight.

"What happens if a cop beats my ass and I file a complaint?" demanded one. "Whose word does the judge take?"

"The judge takes the evidence and evaluates it objectively and comes to a decision."

"Yeah, but it's usually two cops against one of

us, and if both testify against me, what happens? Do
you think the judge is going to listen to me?''

"Bring some witnesses."

"That ain't going to do anything."

"That's your problem. If you don't like the legal
system in this country, work to change it."

"Okay man," one fellow said to Gain, "You pretty
smart. If I smack my buddy here upside the head and
he files a complaint, what you gonna do?''

"Arrest you."

"Cool. Now let's say one of your ugly cops smacks
me upside the head and I file a complaint—what you
gonna do?''

"Investigate the complaint, and if there's anything to it, why we'll take action—probably suspend
him."

"Why do *we* get arrested and *you* investigated?''

The deputy chief's response was that most private
companies with internal difficulties don't want to be investigated by outside agencies. The fellows retorted:
"Police are *not* a private business. You're supposed to
work for the people!''

"And shit, you cats get to carry guns. No businessman carries guns. It's a different scene, man."

"How come you got all kinds of squad cars in this
neighborhood every night? And have two and three
cops in each of them?''

"The crime rate is high in this area," replied Gain,
"and we get a lot of calls and complaints about it."

"Yeah, and you smart enough to know that when
you come around here, you better be wearing helmets
and carrying shotguns. If you that clever, you got to
be smart enough to handle your own goddamn cops.

At this point the fellows all jumped on the deputy
chief the same way they had jumped on the sergeant
the day before:

"Why don't you just let us run our own damn community?"

"Yeah. There should be people on the force who've been in jail because they the only people who know what it means to be busted. People in West Oakland should be police because they know their community; you don't."

"Why do we get all the speeding tickets?"

"How come we got to fight in Vietnam?"

"Why the judges so hard on us? They don't treat white cats—I mean dudes—the way they do us."

The chief began assembling his papers and stood up. "You guys aren't interested in talking. You want to yell. When you want to talk, come down to my office and if I'm free we'll talk."

But the fellows had the last word. While he was leaving they peppered him with gibes about how *they* were tired of talking; promised to dynamite his office; and called the police chief a coward for not coming down to speak with them.

When the deputy chief had gone, the instructor asked the fellows why they insisted on ganging up on people like the police. The answer provides a lot of insight into the young men's actions toward the police, businessmen, and public officials:

"These people just trying to run a game on us. If we give them time to think about answers, they gonna put us in a trick. We've *got* to gang up on them because they gang up on us. Did you dig the way that cat brought three other cats with him? Besides, how else could we put them down?"

A subtle form of racism

In effect, the young men had inverted the meaning and aims of the TIDE program. It was supposed to be an opportunity for them to plan careers and prepare themselves for their life's work. The immediate goal was to help them get started by showing them how to get a job. The youngsters had a different view. The program was a way to play some games and take some outings—an interesting diversion from the boredom and frustration of ghetto life in the summer. In some respects it was also a means of confronting, on equal terms, high-status people normally unavailable to them —and of venting on them their anger and hostility. But primarily they saw it as a $5-a-day job.

The program simply did not meet the needs of these young men. In fact, it was not really meant to. The Great Society was trying to "run a game on" black youth. TIDE asked them to stop being what they are. It tried to lead them into white middle-class America by showing that America was interested in getting them jobs. But America does not provide many jobs—let alone attractive jobs—for those with police records, with few skills, with black skins. The youths knew that; TIDE workers knew that, too. They did not train youths for work, but tried to make them believe that if they knew *how* to get a job, they could. The young men saw through the sham.

Ironically, the view that Negro youths, rather than society, are responsible for the employment problem is very similar to the familiar line of white racism. Negroes will not work because they are lazy and shiftless, the old Southern bigot would say. The Northern liberal today would put it a little differently: Negroes cannot get jobs because of their psychological and cultural impediments; what they need is cultural improvement, a proper attitude, the ability to sell themselves. Both views suggest that inequities in the job and opportunity structure of America are minor compared to the deficiencies of Negroes themselves. In the end, Northern liberals and Southern racists agree: The problem is mainly with Negroes, not with our society. This fallacy underlies much of the war on poverty's approach and is indicative of the subtle forms racism is taking in America today.

RACIAL UNREST

BY GEORGE S. SCHUYLER

The current crop of anti-white disturbances, like those in the past, is the inevitable consequence of the increasing competition between rival civil rights groups led by career agitators vying for the profits of organized pandemonium. Never have so many innocent people been betrayed by so few for so little.

There are as many different kinds of Negroes as there are white people, and most of them deplore the bad reputation they have been given by the excesses of the agitational and criminal elements of their so-called race. They respect life and property. They own millions of homes, automobiles and modern utensils and do not cram the jails. Like their white peers, they are eager to live in peace. They have no illusions about the marching, mobbing, picketing, vandalizing Negro element. They know there is a lot of law in the end of a policeman's nightstick, and they want it used.

George S. Schuyler has been a reporter and editor for various Negro newspapers and magazines for over 40 years.

"Racial Unrest" originally appeared in newspapers throughout the country. Copyright 1965 by North American Newspaper Alliance; reprinted by permission.

Above all, these Negroes wish white people in authority would stop flattering and encouraging the sorcerer's apprentices leading astray the mentally retarded and criminally-bent black minority.

Utilizing the traditional techniques of "spontaneous" disorder, well known to Communists, Nazis and other political perverts, the self-appointed leaders of the Negro revolution have for years recklessly incited young Negroes to mass action inside (and often outside) the urban Negro enclaves.

In turn, they have denounced "police brutality," "the white power structure," "residential segregation," "*de facto* segregated schools," "job discrimination," "phony white liberals," and a whole gamut of grievances which could not possibly be solved or even ameliorated in a century, if then, and will never lessen racial conflict.

Constant suggestions of "a long hot summer" and "conditions getting worse before they get better," are but invitations to hoodlums, arsonists and vandals, aided by white beatnik amoralists and malcontent leftists currently disturbing our campuses.

Not a single one of these trumpeted evils is nonexistent here nor in any other country similarly circumstanced. They are products of our color caste system which will never be improved by Negro insurrection. They are in all multi-racial and multi-ethnic societies from Soviet Muslim Asia to central Africa. These problems are more agitated here because the United States has been a sitting duck for left-wing moralizers who have made millions of well-meaning Americans feel like Nazi racists, and who have persuaded gullible Negroes into believing the only thing holding them back is persecution.

Only the most self-serving demagogues, arrogant know-it-alls, or men with social revolution in mind would stir up a social situation so fraught with tragedy for Negroes, or profess to believe that any predominant social class would willingly surrender power, prestige and privileges in the face of threats and violent demonstrations.

Ever since the long and futile Montgomery bus boycott (settled not by marching but by federal court order), the posse of political parsons in the Southern Christian Leadership Conference (SCLC) have roamed the country collecting coin and infecting the mentally retarded with the germs of civil disobedience, camouflaged as non-violence and love of white people.

Phony prayers for the salvation of white "oppressors" and chanting slave songs fooled nobody except possibly the utopians and wishful thinkers. Only the unwary and True Believers thought this program was anything but pixilated.

As many Negroes foresaw, the net result of this long encouragement of civil disobedience, disdain for authority and general disrespect for public morals was to set the stage for the successive disgraceful orgies of burning, looting, vandalism and death, with the criminal elements of the slum proletariat taking over. Ironically, when police called upon these civil rights leaders to help control the rampaging mobs, they were, if found, completely ineffective.

With the recklessness of complete ignorance or irresponsibility, the Southern Christian Leadership Conference sent its mobile gangs of young clergymen from place to place to take over the revolution despite expressed objections of local leaders, even mobilizing school children to face police clubs, dogs and fire hoses, breeding ill will and jeopardizing Negro jobs by promotion of nuisance tactics.

James Farmer, the professional pacifist and war resister who heads the Congress of Racial Equality, has played an even more sinister role with outright challenges to law, order and public peace. Like SCLC,

this outfit operates schools of subversion where gradu-
ates are trained how to march on city halls and court
houses, fall limp when arrested, and in other ways
make pests of themselves.

Not to be outdone by these competitors for the
scarce civil rights dollar, the veteran National Association for the Advancement of Colored People (NAACP)
saw the expedience of adopting the same tactics of boycotts, sit-ins, marches and picketings. It even went
much farther by thinking up the *de facto* school segregation gimmick which has kept the North and East
in an uproar for the last three years.

The empty assumption behind this campaign is
that schools predominantly attended by Negro children are *ipso facto* segregated and therefore inferior;
and that to equalize public education this "imbalance"
must be corrected by moving the Negro children into
predominantly "white" schools. Since this was and is
obviously impossible, what small victories have attended these Herculean efforts have been pyrrhic. Nowhere have school boycotts, marches and besiegements
of boards of education done else but worsen race relations.

All of these civil rights leaders have joined in a
loud chorus denouncing "police brutality" or the force-
ful suppression of crime which flourishes in every large
Negro community. Every subordinate from coast to
coast joined in the hue and cry, although decent Negroes as well as whites suffer from this criminal element.

The cry sounds in many cities, with monotonous
regularity, for "civilian review boards" to help wreck
discipline and restrain the police from doing what they
are hired to do. This outcry has emboldened the
Negro criminal element and lowered its respect for and
fear of the police.

The respectable bulk of Negroes has been reduced to silence by the terrorism of the agitational element. Every Negro who has openly opposed its illegal and senseless actions has been denounced as an "Uncle Tom," an enemy of his people and lackey of the whites.

One distinguished and authentic Negro leader, the Rev. Dr. Joseph E. Jackson, president of the five-million-strong National Baptist Convention (NBC) of America, Inc., was hooted off the stand in Chicago's stadium because he expressed views opposed to those of the professional agitators. The current president of the Philadelphia branch of the NAACP has had a field day denouncing the conservative middle-class Negroes in the organization.

Craven politicians have contributed much to this insurrectionary atmosphere by not standing up to the intellectual authors of violence and subversion. Consider the spectacle of New York's Mayor Robert F. Wagner skulking through the basement of New York's City Hall rather than have thrown out the beatniks picketing his office, of other high officials permitting their work to be disrupted in the name of civil rights; of needed public construction being halted by CORE beatniks; of President Johnson being booed at the New York World's Fair. The "power structure" has been long-suffering but much too cooperative for its own good.

Most of the civil rights leaders who have sparked these insurrections would still be unknown if it had not been for the mass communications media which publicized them on every occasion, put them on innumerable television programs and wrote profiles of them, as if they wanted this racket to succeed. At the same time newspapers, magazines, radio and television sought out not a single Negro with an opposing viewpoint. It is hard to remember such a one-sided presentation.

Just prior to the Los Angeles shambles, a local radio station had on one of its programs an ex-criminal, Charlie Sims, head of the gun-carrying Louisiana Deacons for Defense and Justice. Undoubtedly tens of thousands of Los Angeles Negroes heard and applauded him.

When returning Gov. Brown of California described the Los Angeles shambles as "a state of siege" he spoke aptly. President Johnson expressed horror over the bloody orgy but did not speculate on the causes of it all. To find the source he needed to look no farther than the Negro civil rights leaders with whom he has frequently conferred, especially when they promised to suspend demonstrations until after the 1964 election.

Now that the civil rights law of 1965 and the voting rights law are operative, he and everybody else had a right to expect that we would see an end to demonstrations, picketing, arson, looting and vandalism. But these evils are easier started than stopped, and they just don't go away because another law is on the books.

What this country badly needs is public officials who will not temporize with illegality and disorder garbed in the mantle of civil rights and equality; who will suppress crime and violence regardless of color; judges who will act with speed and vigor to jail disturbers of the peace; and a more responsible communications media that will refrain from persistently exciting the idle, envious and lawless.

WHY REBELS
ON THE CAMPUS

BY THOMAS O'BRIEN

I am a student nigger. It is an appropriate term. I am not black by skin, but black because my university considers me a second class citizen.

This spring I participated in a sit-in at Colgate University with 500 other students and 40 members of the faculty. It preceded the police riot at Columbia, was completely nonviolent and resulted in no destruction of property. The president of the university characterized the sit-in as a "religious experience."

In the eyes of the majority of students, alumni and observers, these virtues are insufficient. In the eyes of the American public, any disturbance at any college is reason to suspect subversion. This is fundamentally the same reaction that met the first civil rights marches. When students or black people raise their voice, it is

Thomas W. O'Brien, a sophomore at Colgate University, is a George W. Cobb Fellow and the leader of Coalition for a New Colgate.

"Why Rebels on the Campus" originally appeared in America *(October 5, 1968),* © America, *National Catholic Weekly, New York, N.Y., and is reprinted by permission.*

presumed that some outside agitators ("bad niggers," like Dr. King or Stokely Carmichael) have been up to some mischief.

The American stereotype of the student is breaking down, fundamentally because the values of today's intellectual elite are very different from those of their parents. The old convenient notions—that we would go on swallowing goldfishes and staging orgies at Fort Lauderdale for CBS, or, on the other hand, quietly memorizing Latin verbs in a corner—have been shattered by the serious politicking of the New Left.

We are no longer the nice kids for whom Mom, Dad and the Prudential agent have sweated for years. We will do no stepin' fetchit for the board of trustees, answer no "yes boss" to the administration, eat no slice of academic watermelon, obey no directive of the United States government—unless, of course, it is right. To the disciples of Sen. Joe McCarthy, whose crusading paranoia has been transmitted to an entire generation of middle class Americans, we obviously appear subversive.

There were no Communists at Colgate, and I suspect Gus Hall would have been laughed at by the demonstrators at Columbia. There were 35 black students, the campus association of black collegians (ABC), who shook us from moral apathy in a time of need. In a society based upon individual appropriation, this is definitely subversive.

What happened at Colgate is microcosmic. It symbolized the possibility of black-white solidarity in this country. It prefigures greater struggle, for our eventual aim has become the elimination of the power of the board of trustees. It is a shocking concept, a democratic concept.

The immediate issue of the sit-in was discrimination in fraternities. One fraternity, Phi Delta Theta, had this year "blackballed" a Jewish freshman who desired to get into the house. In March the student senate expelled Phi Delta Theta from its membership.

In 1954 the student senate voted to eliminate racial discrimination in selective living units. The same year, the board of trustees declared that there would be no time limit within which this reform was to be carried out, or, in other words, that there would be no reform. Since then, the trustees have taken no action to end discrimination.

Under the emotional stress of the death of Dr. King, many of us felt the time had come for *someone* to do *something*. There is a quality of immediacy about the whole student nigger movement. This is not because we are impatient or impulsive, but rather because every legal channel has been tried and found to be a dead end. Rap Brown worked for years in the Student Nonviolent Co-ordinating Committee and saw minimal gains and maximum suffering for his people. The harshness of his voice is only a response to the harshness of the massacre at Selma.

The Negro has been told for years that the better life will come tomorrow, that reforms would come slowly, that he had to wait. But he has to live today; his children have to be fed today. Likewise, I have to live with my conscience today; I must live with the guilt of genocide today. In the act of brotherhood there is no "tomorrow"; in the act of openness there is only today.

Certainly the physical needs of the Negro living in a ghetto are not mine. Those, however, who cannot understand the force of my moral need simply do not understand morality. They have been raised on a gospel of materialism and self-procurement; "openness" and "brotherhood" are platitudes they hear at church.

On the first day of the demonstration at Colgate, Elwood Berry, a former student and the founder of

ABC, struck to the heart of the issue: "This country is not going to be allowed to live with a lie in its mouth. We are confronted this morning with some more promises. But how many promises have we heard? 'All men are created equal.' You're lying. We're going to straighten this country out because *you* don't have the moral fiber to straighten it out."

Such statements do not make black-white solidarity very easy, but they do stir the apathetic conscience. The challenge at Colgate was to show 35 black Americans that the white race was not living a lie.

The lie says black men are just as good as white men ("But certainly not in our fraternity system, or our neighborhood, or our family circle"); the lie says this is a Christian country, a somewhat moral country ("But you can't expect us to pay taxes to eliminate poverty"); the lie says violence is wrong ("But surely we are justified in napalming Vietnam"); the lie says America is a land of opportunity ("But let's not move too fast in providing jobs and housing"). The lie says freedom, but the liars deny freedom; the lie says peace, but the liars make war; and the lie multiplies in dishonesty when the liars fail to face the immorality of their lie. We have all lied, students no less than their parents, New Leftists no less so than the Old Right. The only distinguishing quality is that some of us, occasionally, have the courage to believe quite literally that the truth will set us free.

The lie is spoken to the student nigger as well. He is told he is being trained to live and work in a democratic society, while the university remains dictatorial in its power structure. He is given the sop of a student senate only to discover that all the real decisions are handed down from the trustees, absentee plutocrats whose conception of moral courage is limited to the stock market and Sunday school. Spending only a few days at the university each year, they are allowed to make judgments upon problems they are completely unfamiliar with. It is as though the United States was governed by an American businessman who spent all his time in Europe.

The fraternity issue at Colgate has crystallized the deeper issue of whether or not the university will be a democracy or an autocracy. It is the board of trustees that has consistently opposed the manifest will of the students in the issue of discrimination. It is the board of trustees that now opposes the "open housing" position taken by the student senate after the sit-in, and by the faculty by a vote of 72 to 19. Consequently, "open housing" will not be put into effect, that is, until the board of trustees is deprived, forcefully if necessary, of its dictatorial power.

Elwood Berry articulated the growing hostility between the demonstrators and the trustees. On the third night of the sit-in, he said: "All those cats cared about was that they go out of this with as little skin off their noses as possible. All that matters to them is that they lose as little money as possible. You don't mean a damn thing. You're black now. You know now. You're black. You know what it means for a system to look at you and ask: 'What's the matter? You never had it so good.' You're black now. Carry it home with you, baby. Savor it. Understand it. Take it home."

Certainly not every college student considers himself to be black in this sense of the word. Certainly not even a majority are inclined to sit-in in behalf of any cause; certainly less than that number in behalf of human brotherhood. The sit-ins invariably occur at Eastern liberal arts colleges, and the demonstrators are invariably studying the humanities. But the vast wasteland of technicians, engineers and business majors is not responsive to the call for truth.

The American educational system has succeeded in producing moral nonentities, robots who neatly fit into the pattern of materialism, groomed and clean to walk out of fraternity row directly onto Wall Street. They are trained for this life by their years of subservience in high school and college. They have been trained to enter a society that is superficially democratic, formally democratic, but fundamentally conformist and socially totalitarian.

A democracy does not consist of ballot boxes and the parliamentary process. It must be animated by a democratic spirit, which is self-sacrificial and courageous. The spirit of democracy requires openness and sharing, and that involves a good degree of unselfishness. But this society, for which the university serves as basic training, is geared to individual appropriation. By definition, a selfish society cannot be democratic.

The second element in the democratic spirit is courage: courage to participate, courage to dissent, courage to serve the community *in truth*, courage to challenge power, courage to take power when that is necessary, courage to be democratic. When we sat-in at Colgate we acted in that spirit, in the conviction that something had to be done, whether or not the trustees approved.

The basic point is this: that the university, which is undemocratic in its power structure, prepares the individual for a society that is undemocratic in its spirit. The hundreds of students at Colgate who said they were sympathetic to the aims of the sit-in, but who disapproved of the means being used, had been taught well, taught to resist the lessons of their books, taught to be good niggers. They join the ranks of the passive, the cynical and the selfish, along with all the business majors from Indiana.

We were called a "radical anarchist movement out to destroy Colgate." I am sure that many red-blooded Americans have the same attitude toward the peace marchers and civil rights agitators. We are all collectively accused of by-passing democratic procedures, for we do not abide by the will of the majority.

Moral dissent and the forms it takes must not be limited by the mores of the herd. We have the example of Thomas More and Socrates, subversives in their time, to guide us; we have the groundwork philosophy of existentialism to strengthen our notions of individualism; we have the memory of Dr. King to compel our sense of justice. According to society, since he broke laws, he too was an enemy to democracy.

In another sense, the New Left does abide by the will of the majority. Of those who *care*, of those who are politically conscious, of those who just might someday join the Peace Corps, of those who make the dean's list, we are by far the majority. We are the ones who responded to John Kennedy's call, who asked what we could do for our country, and who were answered with war and racism. We are the ones who made Gene McCarthy more than a dreamer, his candidacy more than a dream. And we will not be deterred from the revolution in values that must sweep this country.

We are told we are disrupting academic life; we say that academic life, like democracy, cannot be something defined in terms of procedures. On a superficial level, we have certainly made life difficult for the dean and interrupted the classroom schedule. But on a deeper level, demonstrations to secure human dignity, to end war, to fight injustice, are most in keeping with the *spirit* of learning.

Bad student niggers are not in college, like many of our parents, in order to add an A.B. to our name; we are not concerned with a $10,000 income to validate our degree. We are not interested in studying ethics or studying a philosophy, but in *living* ethically and *living* philosophically. We recognize no separation between life and intellect, and consequently we do not consider it "disruption" to put the two together.

In sitting-in for the cause of humanity, we have not negated our studies, but made them radically alive and operative. We have removed them from an ivory tower, just as the Council removed the Christian doctrine of love from the security of the altar. But like the conservative cardinals, the American establishment sees the deepening of meaning as a prostitution.

Furthermore, although many of us have embraced nonviolence as a philosophy, many of our brothers have not. Yet if one values consistency, it is impossible to condemn violence in internal dissent if at the same time violence is condoned as a means of keeping international order. Lyndon Johnson, one of the leading spokesmen of liberal-speak contradictions, overlooked this consistency when he called for people of this country to put down their arms while he was busy depopulating towns and villages in Southeast Asia.

This is not intended as a threat, but as an explication of fact. There are going to be more demonstrations in behalf of human rights, more sit-ins on college campuses, and some of them, given the violent example of our leaders, will inevitably bring violence. If the American public finds violence so shocking, let them remember that the cornerstone in our national defense is the nuclear ability to overkill the world three times.

The question to be asked is not whether or not there will be trouble on college campuses throughout the next few years. At Colgate, the trouble existed for many decades, obscured and hidden. The "troublemakers" are not civil rights agitators or New Leftists, but the agents of injustice, the cynical and the apathetic. There will be trouble as long as they are the formulators of policy.

In the long run, the educational system in this country bears in itself the seeds of its own destruction. The possibility of educating more young people makes certain the creation of more radicals. The process begins only with a trickle (just as in 1950 there were only a few bad niggers around), but soon like a snowball, it begins to grow and gain momentum. It must look frightening from the bottom of the hill; perhaps America is not so wrong in its apprehensiveness.

Student niggers are irresponsible. We are not worried about the mortgage and the tax surcharge; we are out of Mom's and Dad's control, and yet free from the responsibility of family. We are not yet corrupted by the financial responsibilities of this self-centered society.

In that sense, we are more responsible, free to respond openly to a brother, free to assume directly on our shoulders the responsibility for the survival of the world. The society's conception of responsibility is limited to bounded areas: self, family, community, country. We have freed it from its bounds. We are responsible to all mankind. And with that responsibility, *we ain't gonna say "yes boss" no more.* That would be a lie, too.

REBELS WITHOUT A PROGRAM

BY GEORGE F. KENNAN

There is an ideal that has long been basic to the learning process as we have known it, one that stands at the very center of our modern institutions of higher education and that had its origin, I suppose, in the clerical and monastic character of the medieval university. It is the ideal of the association of the process of learning with a certain remoteness from the contemporary scene—a certain detachment and seclusion, a certain voluntary withdrawal and renunciation of participation in contemporary life in the interests of the achievement of a better perspective on that life when the period of withdrawal is over. It is an ideal that does not predicate any total conflict between thought and action, but recognizes that there is a time for each.

No more striking, or moving, description of this ideal has ever come to my attention than that which

George F. Kennan, former Ambassador to Russia, is a professor at the Institute for Advanced Study, Princeton, New Jersey.

was given by Woodrow Wilson in 1896 at the time of the Princeton Sesquicentennial.

"I have had sight," Wilson said, "of the perfect place of learning in my thought: a free place, and a various, where no man could be and not know with how great a destiny knowledge had come into the world—itself a little world; but not perplexed, living with a singleness of aim not known without; the home of sagacious men, hardheaded and with a will to know, debaters of the world's questions every day and used to the rough ways of democracy; and yet a place removed—calm Science seated there, recluse, ascetic, like a nun; not knowing that the world passes, not caring, if the truth but come in answer to her prayer. . . . A place where ideals are kept in heart in an air they can breathe; but no fool's paradise. A place where to hear the truth about the past and hold debate about the affairs of the present, with knowledge and without passion; like the world in having all men's life at heart, a place for men and all that concerns them; but unlike the world in its self-possession, its thorough way of talk, its care to know more than the moment brings to light; slow to take excitement, its air pure and wholesome with a breath of faith; every eye within it bright in the clear day and quick to look toward heaven for the confirmation of its hope. Who shall show us the way to this place?"

There is a dreadful incongruity between this vision and the state of mind—and behavior—of the radical left on the American campus today. In place of a calm science, "recluse, ascetic, like a nun," not knowing or caring that the world passes "if the truth but come in answer to her prayer," we have people utterly absorbed in the affairs of this passing world. And instead of these affairs being discussed with knowledge and without passion, we find them treated with transports of passion and with a minimum, I fear, of knowledge. In place of slowness to take excitement, we have a readiness to react emotionally, and at once, to a great variety of issues. In place of self-possession, we have screaming tantrums and brawling in the streets. In place of the "thorough way of talk" that Wilson envisaged, we have banners and epithets and obscenities and virtually meaningless slogans. And in place of bright eyes "looking to heaven for the confirmation of their hope," we have eyes glazed with anger and passion, too often dimmed as well by artificial abuse of the psychic structure that lies behind them, and looking almost everywhere else but to heaven for the satisfaction of their aspirations.

I quite understand that those who espouse this flagrant repudiation of the Wilsonian ideal constitute only a minority on any campus. But tendencies that represent the obsession of only a few may not be without partial appeal, at certain times, and within certain limits, to many others. If my own analysis is correct, there are a great many students who may resist any complete surrender to these tendencies, but who nevertheless find them intensely interesting, are to some extent attracted or morally bewildered by them, find themselves driven, in confrontation with them, either into various forms of pleasing temptation, on the one hand, or into crises of conscience, on the other.

If I see them correctly (and I have no pretensions to authority on this subject), there are two dominant tendencies among the people I have here in mind, and superficially they would seem to be in conflict one with the other. On the one side there is angry militancy, full of hatred and intolerance and often quite prepared to embrace violence as a source of change. On the other side there is gentleness, passivity, quietism—ostensibly a yearning for detachment from the affairs of the world, not the detachment Woodrow Wilson had in mind, for that was one intimately and

sternly related to the real world, the objective, external
world, whereas this one takes the form of an attempt
to escape into a world which is altogether illusory and
subjective.

What strikes one first about the angry militancy is
the extraordinary degree of certainty by which it is in-
spired: certainty of one's own rectitude, certainty of
the correctness of one's own answers, certainty of the
accuracy and profundity of one's own analysis of the
problems of contemporary society, certainty as to the
iniquity of those who disagree. Of course, vehemence of
feeling and a conviction that right is on one's side have
seldom been absent from the feelings of politically excited youth. But somehow or other they seem particularly out of place at just this time. Never has there been
an era when the problems of public policy even ap-
proached in their complexity those by which our society
is confronted today, in this age of technical innovation
and the explosion of knowledge. The understanding of
these problems is something to which one could well
give years of disciplined and restrained study, years of
the scholar's detachment, years of readiness to reserve
judgment while evidence is being accumulated. And
this being so, one is struck to see such massive certain-
ties already present in the minds of people who not only
have not studied very much but presumably *are not*
studying a great deal, because it is hard to imagine
that the activities to which this aroused portion of our
student population gives itself are ones readily com-
patible with quiet and successful study.

The world seems to be full, today, of embattled
students. The public prints are seldom devoid of the
record of their activities. Photographs of them may be
seen daily: screaming, throwing stones, breaking windows, overturning cars, being beaten or dragged about
by police and, in the case of those on other continents,
burning libraries. That these people are embattled is

unquestionable. That they are really students, I must be permitted to doubt. I have heard it freely confessed by members of the revolutionary student generation of Tsarist Russia that, proud as they were of the revolutionary exploits of their youth, they never really learned anything in their university years; they were too busy with politics. The fact of the matter is that the state of being *enragé* is simply incompatible with fruitful study. It implies a degree of existing emotional and intellectual commitment which leaves little room for open-minded curiosity.

I am not saying that students should not be concerned, should not have views, should not question what goes on in the field of national policy and should not voice their questions about it. Some of us, who are older, share many of their misgivings, many of their impulses. Some of us have no less lively a sense of the dangers of the time, and are no happier than they are about a great many things that are now going on. But it lies within the power as well as the duty of all of us to recognize not only the possibility that we might be wrong but the virtual certainty that on some occasions we are bound to be. The fact that this is so does not absolve us from the duty of having views and putting them forward. But it does make it incumbent upon us to recognize the element of doubt that still surrounds the correctness of these views. And if we do that, we will not be able to lose ourselves in transports of moral indignation against those who are of opposite opinion and follow a different line; we will put our views forward only with a prayer for forgiveness for the event that we prove to be mistaken.

I am aware that inhibitions and restraints of this sort on the part of us older people would be attributed by many members of the student left to a sweeping corruption of our moral integrity. Life, they would hold, has impelled us to the making of compromises;

and these compromises have destroyed the usefulness of our contribution. Crippled by our own cowardice, prisoners of the seamy adjustments we have made in order to be successfully a part of the American establishment, we are regarded as no longer capable of looking steadily into the strong clear light of truth.

In this, as in most of the reproaches with which our children shower us, there is of course an element of justification. There is a point somewhere along the way in most of our adult lives, admittedly, when enthusiasms flag, when idealism becomes tempered, when responsibility to others, and even affection for others, compels greater attention to the mundane demands of private life. There is a point when we are even impelled to place the needs of children ahead of the dictates of a defiant idealism, and to devote ourselves, pusillanimously, if you will, to the support and rearing of these same children—precisely in order that at some future date they may have the privilege of turning upon us and despising us for the materialistic faint-heartedness that made their maturity possible. This, no doubt, is the nature of the compromise that millions of us make with the imperfections of government and society in our time. Many of us could wish that it might have been otherwise—that the idealistic pursuit of public causes might have remained our exclusive dedication down into later life.

But for the fact that this is not so I cannot shower myself or others with reproaches. I have seen more harm done in this world by those who tried to storm the bastions of society in the name of utopian beliefs, who were determined to achieve the elimination of all evil and the realization of the millennium within their own time, than by all the humble efforts of those who have tried to create a little order and civility and affection within their own intimate entourage, even at the cost of tolerating a great deal of evil in the public domain. Behind this modesty, after all, there has been the recognition of a vitally important truth—a truth that the Marxists, among others, have never brought themselves to recognize; namely, that the decisive seat of evil in this world is not in social and political institutions, and not even, as a rule, in the ill will or iniquities of statesmen, but simply in the weakness and imperfection of the human soul itself, and by that I mean literally every soul, including my own and that of the student militant at the gates. For this reason, as Tocqueville so clearly perceived when he visited this country 130 years ago, the success of a society may be said, like charity, to begin at home.

So much, then, for the angry ones. Now, a word about the others: the quiescent ones, the hippies and the flower people.

In one sense, my feeling for these people is one of pity, not unmixed, in some instances, with horror. I am sure that they want none of this pity. They would feel that it comes to them for the wrong reasons. If they feel sorry for themselves, it is because they see themselves as the victims of a harsh, hypocritical, and unworthy adult society. If I feel sorry for them, it is because I see them as the victims of certain great and destructive philosophic errors.

One of these errors—and it is one that affects particularly those who take drugs, but not those alone—is the belief that the human being has marvelous resources within himself that can be released and made available to him merely by the passive submission to certain sorts of stimuli: by letting esthetic impressions of one sort or another roll over him or by letting his psychic equilibrium be disoriented by chemical agencies that give him the sensation of experiencing tremendous things. Well, it is true that human beings sometimes have marvelous resources within themselves. It is also true that these resources are capable, ideally,

of being released and made available to the man that
harbors them and through him to others, and sometimes are so released. But it is not true that they can
be released by hippie means.

It is only through effort, through doing, through
action—never through passive experience—that man
grows creatively. It is only by volition and effort that
he becomes fully aware of what he has in him of
creativity and becomes capable of embodying it, of
making it a part of himself, of communicating it to
others. There is no pose more fraudulent—and students would do well to remember this when they look
at each other—than that of the individual who pre-
tends to have been exalted and rendered more im-
pressive by his communion with some sort of inner
voice whose revelations he is unable to describe or to
enact. And particularly is this pose fraudulent when
the means he has chosen to render himself susceptible to this alleged revelation is the deliberate disori-
entation of his own psychic system; for it may be said
with surety that any artificial intervention of this sort—
into the infinitely delicate balance that nature created
in the form of man's psychic make-up—produces its
own revenge, takes its own toll, proceeds at the cost of
the true creative faculties and weakens rather than
strengthens.

The second error I see in the outlook of these
people is the belief in the possibility and validity of a
total personal permissiveness. They are misjudging,
here, the innermost nature of man's estate. There is not,
and cannot be, such a thing as total freedom. The normal needs and frailties of the body, not to mention the
elementary demands of the soul itself, would rule that
out if nothing else did. But *beyond* that, any freedom
*from something implies a freedom to something. And
because our reality is a complex one,* in which conflicts
of values are never absent, there can be no advance

toward any particular objective, not even the pursuit of pleasure, that does not imply the sacrifice of other possible objectives. Freedom, for this reason, is definable only in terms of the obligations and restraints and sacrifices it accepts. It exists, as a concept, only in relationship to something else which is by definition its opposite; and that means commitment, duty, self-restraint.

Every great artist has known this. Every great philosopher has recognized it. It has lain at the basis of Judaic-Christian teaching. Tell me what framework of discipline you are prepared to accept, and I will attempt to tell you what freedom might mean for you. But if you tell me that you are prepared to accept no framework of discipline at all, then I will tell you, as Dostoevski told his readers, that you are destined to become the most unfree of men; for freedom begins only with the humble acceptance of membership in, and subordination to, a natural order of things, and it grows only with struggle, and self-discipline, and faith.

To shun the cruelty and corruption of this world is one thing. It is not always unjustifiable. Not everyone is made to endure these things. There is something to be said for the cultivation, by the right people, and in the right way, of the virtues of detachment, of withdrawal, of unworldliness, of innocence and purity, if you will. That, as a phase of life, is just what Wilson was talking about. In an earlier age, those who are now the flower children and the hippies would perhaps have entered monastic life or scholarly life or both. But there, be it noted, they would very definitely have accepted a framework of discipline, and it would normally have been a very strict one. If it was a monastic order, their lives would have been devoted to the service of God and of other men, not of themselves and their senses. If it was the world of scholarship, their lives would have been devoted to the pursuit of truth,

which never comes easily or without discipline and sacrifice. They would have accepted an obligation to cultivate order, not chaos; cleanliness, not filth; self-abnega-
tion, not self-indulgence; health, not demoralization.

Now I have indicated that I pity these people,
and in general I do. But sometimes I find it hard to
pity them, because they themselves are sometimes so
pitiless. There is, in this cultivation of an absolute freedom, and above all in the very self-destructiveness with
which it often expresses itself, a selfishness, a hard-
heartedness, a callousness, an irresponsibility, an indifference to the feelings of others, that is its own condemnation. No one ever destroys just himself alone.
Such is the network of intimacy in which every one of
us is somehow embraced, that whoever destroys himself destroys to some extent others as well. Many of
these people prattle about the principle of love; but
their behavior betrays this principle in the most elementary way. Love—and by that I mean the receiving
of love as well as the bestowal of it—is itself an obligation, and as such is incompatible with the quest for a
perfect freedom. Just the cruelty to parents alone, which
is implicit in much of this behavior, is destructive of
the purest and most creative form of love that does exist
or could exist in this mortal state.

And one would like to warn these young people
that in distancing themselves so recklessly not only
from the wisdom but from the feelings of parents, they
are hacking at their own underpinnings—and even
those of people as yet unborn. There could be no
greater illusion than the belief that one can treat one's
parents unfeelingly and with contempt and yet expect
that one's own children will some day treat one otherwise; for such people break the golden chain of affection that binds the generations and gives continuity and
meaning to life.

One cannot, therefore, on looking at these young

people in all the glory of their defiant rags and hairdos, always just say, with tears in one's eyes: "There goes a tragically wayward youth, striving romantically to document his rebellion against the hypocrisies of the age." One has sometimes to say, and not without indignation: "There goes a perverted and willful and stony-hearted youth by whose destructiveness we are all, in the end, to be damaged and diminished."

These people also pose a problem in the quality of their citizenship. One thing they all seem to have in common—the angry ones as well as the quiet ones—is a complete rejection of, or indifference to, the political system of this country. The quiet ones turn their backs upon it, as though it did not concern them. The angry ones reject it by implication, insofar as they refuse to recognize the validity of its workings or to respect the discipline which, as a system of authority, it unavoidably entails.

I think there is a real error or misunderstanding here. If you accept a democratic system, this means that you are prepared to put up with those of its workings, legislative or administrative, with which you do not agree as well as with those that meet with your concurrence. This willingness to accept, in principle, the workings of a system based on the will of the majority, even when you yourself are in the minority, is simply the essence of democracy. Without it there could be no system of representative self-government at all. When you attempt to alter the workings of the system by means of violence or civil disobedience, this, it seems to me, can have only one of two implications: either you do not believe in democracy at all and consider that society ought to be governed by enlightened minorities such as the one to which you, of course, belong; or you consider that the present system is so imperfect that it is not truly representative, that it no longer serves adequately as a vehicle for the will of the

majority, and that this leaves to the unsatisfied no adequate means of self-expression other than the primitive
one of calling attention to themselves and their emotions by mass demonstrations and mass defiance of established authority. It is surely the latter of these two
implications which we must read from the overwhelming majority of the demonstrations that have recently
taken place.

I would submit that if you find a system inadequate, it is not enough simply to demonstrate indignation and anger over individual workings of it, such
as the persistence of the Vietnam war, or individual
situations it tolerates or fails to correct, such as the
condition of the Negroes in our great cities. If one finds
these conditions intolerable, and if one considers that
they reflect no adequate expression either of the will of
the majority or of that respect for the rights of minorities which is no less essential to the success of any
democratic system, then one places upon one's self, it
seems to me, the obligation of saying in what way this
political system should be modified, or what should be
established in the place of it, to assure that its workings would bear a better relationship to people's needs
and people's feelings.

If the student left had a program of constitutional
amendment or political reform—if it had proposals for
the constructive adaptation of this political system to
the needs of our age—if it was *this* that it was agitating
for, and if its agitation took the form of reasoned argument and discussion, or even peaceful demonstration
accompanied by reasoned argument and discussion—
then many of us, I am sure, could view its protests with
respect, and we would not shirk the obligation, either
to speak up in defense of institutions and national
practices which we have tolerated all our lives, or to
join these young people in the quest for better ones.

But when we are confronted only with violence for violence's sake, and with attempts to frighten or intimidate an administration into doing things for which it can itself see neither the rationale nor the electoral mandate; when we are offered, as the only argument for change, the fact that a number of people are themselves very angry and excited; and when we are presented with a violent objection to what exists, unaccompanied by any constructive concept of what, *ideally,* ought to exist in its place—then we of my generation can only recognize that such behavior bears a disconcerting resemblance to phenomena we have witnessed within our own time in the origins of totalitarianism in other countries, and then we have no choice but to rally to the defense of a public authority with which we may not be in agreement but which is the only one we've got and with which, in some form or another, we cannot conceivably dispense. People should bear in mind that if this—namely noise, violence and lawlessness—is the way they are going to put their case, then many of us who are no happier than they are about some of the policies that arouse their indignation will have no choice but to place ourselves on the other side of the barricades.

These observations reflect a serious doubt whether civil disobedience has any place in a democratic society. But there is one objection I know will be offered to this view. Some people, who accept our political system, believe that they have a right to disregard it and to violate the laws that have flowed from it so long as they are prepared, as a matter of conscience, to accept the penalties established for such behavior.

I am sorry; I cannot agree. The violation of law is not, in the moral and philosophic sense, a privilege that lies offered for sale with a given price tag, like an object in a supermarket, available to anyone who

has the price and is willing to pay for it. It is not like
the privilege of breaking crockery in a tent at the county
fair for a quarter a shot. Respect for the law is not an
obligation which is exhausted or obliterated by willingness to accept the penalty for breaking it.

To hold otherwise would be to place the privilege
of law-breaking preferentially in the hands of the affluent, to make respect for law a commercial proposition
rather than a civic duty and to deny any authority of
law independent of the sanctions established against
its violation. It would then be all right for a man to
create false fire alarms or frivolously to pull the emer-
gency cord on the train, or to do any number of other
things that endangered or inconvenienced other people,
provided only he was prepared to accept the penalties
of so doing. Surely, lawlessness and civil disobedience
cannot be condoned or tolerated on this ground; and
those of us who care for the good order of society have
no choice but to resist attempts at its violation, when
this is their only justification.

Now, being myself a father, I am only too well
aware that people of my generation cannot absolve ourselves of a heavy responsibility for the state of mind in
which these young people find themselves. We are
obliged to recognize here, in the myopia and the crudi-
ties of *their* extremism, the reflection of our own fail-
ings: our smugness, our timidity, our faint-heartedness
and in some instances our weariness, our apathy in the
face of great and obvious evils.

I am also aware that, while their methods may
not be the right ones, and while their discontent may
suffer in its effectiveness from the concentration on
negative goals, the degree of their concern over the
present state of our country and the dangers implicit
in certain of its involvements is by no means exaggerated. This is a time in our national life more serious,

more menacing, more crucial, than any I have ever experienced or ever hoped to experience. Not since the civil conflict of a century ago has this country, as I see it, been in such great danger; and the most excruciating aspect of this tragic state of affairs is that so much of this danger comes so largely from within, where we are giving it relatively little official attention, and so little of it comes, relatively speaking, from the swamps and jungles of Southeast Asia into which we are pouring our treasure of young blood and physical resources.

For these reasons, I do not mean to make light of the intensity of feeling by which this student left is seized. Nor do I mean to imply that people like myself can view this discontent from some sort of smug Olympian detachment, as though it were not our responsibility, as though it were not in part our own ugly and decadent face that we see in this distorted mirror. None of us could have any justification for attempting to enter into communication with these people if we did not recognize, along with the justification for their unhappiness, our own responsibility in the creation of it, and if we did not accompany our appeal to them with a profession of readiness to join them, where they want us to, in the attempt to find better answers to many of these problems.

I am well aware that in approaching them in this way and in taking issue as I have with elements of their outlook and their behavior, it is primarily myself that I have committed, not them. I know that behind all the extremisms—all the philosophical errors, all the egocentricities and all the oddities of dress and deportment—we have to do here with troubled and often pathetically appealing people, acting, however wisely or unwisely, out of sincerity and idealism, out of the unwillingness to accept a meaningless life and a purposeless society.

Well, this is not the life, and not the sort of society, that many of us would like to leave behind us in this country when our work is done. How wonderful it would be, I sometimes think to myself, if we and they—experience on the one hand, strength and enthusiasm on the other—could join forces.

ON LIVING IN A BIOLOGICAL REVOLUTION

BY DONALD FLEMING

Here are a dozen things that we have discovered in the last fifteen years.

1. We have discovered the structure of the genetic substance DNA—the double helix of Watson and Crick—the general nature of the process by which the chromosomal strands are replicated.

2. We have discovered in viruses how to achieve the perfect replication of DNA molecules that are biologically effective.

3. We have discovered the code by which DNA specifies the insertion of amino acids in proteins.

4. We have discovered how to produce hybrid cells between the most diverse vertebrate species, including hybrids between man and mouse; and some of these hybrids have gone on multiplying for several (cellular) generations.

5. We have discovered the power of viruses to invade bacterial and other cells and to insert the genes

Donald Fleming is professor of history at Harvard University.

of the virus into the genome of the host; and we have good reason to conjecture, though not yet to affirm, that this phenomenon is involved in cancer.

6. We have discovered hormonal contraceptives and grasped in principle the strategy for devising a contraceptive pill for *both* sexes, by knocking out certain hormones of the hypothalamus, the master sexual gland of the body.

7. We have discovered on a large scale in the livestock industry that deep-frozen mammalian sperm, suitably mixed with glycerol, can be banked indefinitely and drawn upon as desired to produce viable offspring.

8. We have discovered in human females how to produce superovulation, the release of several eggs into the oviduct at the same time instead of the customary one, with the possibility on the horizon of withdrawing substantial numbers of human eggs for storage, culture in test tubes, or surgical manipulation, without destroying their viability.

9. We have discovered in rabbits how to regulate the sex of offspring by removing fertilized ova from the female before they become implanted in the wall of the uterus, "sexing" the embryos by a technique entailing the deletion of some 200 to 300 cells, flushing embryos of the "wrong" sex down the drain, and then in a substantial minority of cases, successfully reinserting in the uterus embryos of the desired sex that proceed to develop normally.

10. We have discovered drugs, above all the hallucinogens, that simulate psychotic states of mind; and have thereby rendered it plausible that the latter are the product of "inborn errors of metabolism" and as such remediable by the administration of drugs.

11. We have discovered in principle, and to a certain extent in practice, how to repress the immunological "defenses" of the body.

12. We have discovered a combination of immuno-

logical and surgical techniques by which the kidney, liver, or heart can be transplanted with fair prospects of the recipient's survival for months or even years— the first constructive proposal for turning our death wish on the highways to some advantage.

Each of these is a major discovery or complex of discoveries in itself, but they add up to far more than the sum of their parts. They constitute a veritable Biological Revolution likely to be as decisive for the history of the next 150 years as the Industrial Revolution has been for the period since 1750.

Definitions of what constitutes a revolution are legion. An undoctrinaire formulation would be that every full-scale revolution has three main components: a distinctive attitude toward the world; a program for utterly transforming it; and an unshakable, not to say fanatical, confidence that this program can be enacted —a world view, a program, and a faith.

In this sense, Darwinism did not usher in a full-scale biological revolution. Darwinism was a profoundly innovating world view, but one that prescribed no steps to be taken, no victories over nature to be celebrated, no program of triumphs to be successively gained. Indeed, one of the most plausible constructions to be put upon it was that nothing much *could* be done except to submit patiently to the winnowing processes of nature.

This defect was not lost upon Darwin's own cousin Sir Francis Galton, who tried to construct an applied science of eugenics for deliberately selecting out the best human stocks. But Galtonian eugenics was sadly lacking in any authentic biological foundation. Once the science of Mendelian genetics came to general notice about 1900, a more promising form of eugenics began to commend itself, the effort to induce artificial mutation of genes in desirable directions.

This was long the animating faith of one of the

most extraordinary Americans of the twentieth century, the geneticist Hermann J. Muller. He was the actual discoverer, in 1927, of artificial mutation through X rays. But this great achievement, for which he got the Nobel Prize, was a tremendous disappointment to Muller the revolutionary. There was no telling which genes would mutate in which direction, and he came to suspect that the vast majority of mutations were actually harmful in the present situation of the human race.

Muller at the end of his life—he died in 1967—was thrown back upon essentially Galtonian eugenics. He did bring this up to date by his proposal for sperm banks in which the sperm of exceptionally intelligent and socially useful men could be stored for decades and used for artificial insemination. He also envisioned, in the not too distant future, ova banks for storing superior human eggs. But none of these modern touches, these innovations in technique, could conceal the fact that this was still the old eugenics newly garbed, but equally subjective and imprecise.

Biological engineering

The Biological Revolution that Muller failed to bring off was already in progress when he died, but on very different terms from his own. There is a new eugenics in prospect, not the marriage agency kind, but a form of "biological engineering." When this actually comes to pass, chromosomes, segments of chromosomes, and even individual genes will be inserted at will into the genome. Alternatively, germ cells cultured in laboratories will be enucleated and entire tailor-made DNA molecules substituted. Alternatively still, superior genes will be brought into play by hybridization of cells.

The detailed variants upon these general strategies are almost innumerable. They all have in common the fact that they cannot be accomplished at present except in viruses and bacteria or in cell cultures. But it would be a bold man who would dogmatically affirm that none of these possibilities could be brought to bear upon human genetics by the year 2000.

That is a long way off for the firebrands of the Biological Revolution. The Nobel Prize winner Joshua Lederberg in particular has been pushing the claims of a speedier remedy, christened by him "euphenics," and defined as "the engineering of human development." The part of human development that fascinates Lederberg the most is embryology, seen by him as the process of initially translating the instructions coded in the DNA into "the living, breathing organism." Embryology, he says, is "very much in the situation of atomic physics in 1900; having had an honorable and successful tradition it is about to begin!" He thinks it will not take long to mature—"from 5 to no more than 20 years." He adds that most predictions of research progress in recent times have proved to be "far too conservative."

The progress that Lederberg has in mind is the application of new embryological techniques to human affairs. He is at once maddened and obsessed by the nine-months phase in which the human organism has been exempted from experimental and therapeutic intervention—such a waste of time before the scientists can get at us. But the embryo's turn is coming. It would be incredible, he says, "if we did not soon have the basis of developmental engineering technique to regulate, for example, the size of the human brain by prenatal or early postnatal intervention."

Sex control

Nothing as sensational as this has yet been attempted, but the new phase in embryology that Lederberg heralded is undoubtedly getting under way. The most conspicuous figure at present is Robert Edwards of the physiology laboratory at Cambridge University. In 1966 Edwards reported the culture of immature egg cells from the human ovary up to the point of ripeness for fertilization. He made tentative claims to have actually achieved fertilization in test tubes. The incipient hullabaloo in the newspapers about the specter of "test tube babies" led Edwards to clamp a tight lid of security over his researches in progress.

In the spring of this year, however, he and Richard Gardner announced their success in "sexing" fertilized rabbit eggs before implantation in the wall of the uterus and then inducing 20 percent of the reinserted eggs to produce normal full-term infants. The aspect of these findings that attracted general attention, the prospect of regulating the sex of mammalian offspring, is not likely to be of permanent interest. For this purpose, Edwards and Gardner's technique is obviously a clumsy expedient by comparison with predetermining the "sex" of spermatozoa—presently impossible but certainly not inconceivable within the next generation.

The real importance of Edwards and Gardner's work lies elsewhere. They have opened up the possibility of subjecting the early embryo to microsurgery, with the deletion and "inoculation" of cells at the will of the investigator, *and* the production of viable offspring from the results. The manufacture of "chimeras" in the modern biological sense—that is, with genetically distinct cells in the same organism—is clearly in prospect.

Work in this vein has just begun. The only branch

of euphenics that has already become something more than a promising growth stock in science is the suppression of immunological reactions against foreign tissues and the accompanying, highly limited, successes in the transplantation of organs.

Biological revolutionaries

The technical details and immediate prospects in eugenics and euphenics, however fascinating, are less important than the underlying revolutionary temper in biology. The most conspicuous representatives of this temper are Lederberg himself, the biochemical geneticist Edward L. Tatum, and Francis Crick of the model —all of them Nobel Prize winners, with the corresponding leverage upon public opinion. Robert Edwards, though slightly singed by the blast of publicity about test tube babies, is clearly in training for the revolutionary cadre.

One of the stigmata of revolutionaries in any field is their resolute determination to break with traditional culture. For a scientist, the most relevant definition of culture is his own field of research. All of these men would angrily resent being bracketed with biologists in general. Biology has always been a rather loose confederation of naturalists and experimentalists, overlapping in both categories with medical researchers. Today even the pretense that these men somehow constitute a community has been frayed to the breaking point.

At Harvard, for example, the revolutionaries have virtually seceded from the old Biology Department and formed a new department of their own, Biochemistry and Molecular Biology. The younger molecular biologists hardly bother to conceal their contempt for the naturalists, whom they see as old fogies obsequiously attentive to the world as it is rather than bent upon turning it upside down.

In one respect, the molecular biologists do over-lap with the contemporary naturalists and indeed with most creative scientists in general—in their total detachment from religion. In a way, this is a point that could have been made at any time in the last seventy-five years, but with one significant difference. Hermann Muller, for example, born in 1890, had no truck with religion. But he was self-consciously antireligious.

The biological revolutionaries of today are not antireligious but simply unreligious. They give the impression not of defending themselves against religion but of subsisting in a world where that has never been a felt pressure upon them. They would agree with many devout theologians that we are living in a post-Christian world, to such an extent that some of the most doctrinaire biological revolutionaries are able to recognize without embarrassment, and even with a certain gracious condescension, that Christianity did play a useful role in defining the value of the Western world.

The operative word here is in the past tense. Francis Crick says that the facts of science are producing and must produce values that owe nothing to Christianity. "Take," he says, "the suggestion of making a child whose head is twice as big as normal. There is going to be no agreement between Christians and any humanists who lack their particular prejudice about the sanctity of the individual, and who simply want to try it scientifically."

This sense of consciously taking up where religion left off is illuminating in another sense for the revolutionary character of contemporary biology. The parallel is very marked between the original Christian Revolution against the values of the classical world and the Biological Revolution against religious values.

All the great revolutionaries, whether early Christians or molecular biologists, are men of good hope. The future may or may not belong to those who believe in it, but cannot belong to those who don't. Yet at certain points in history, most conspicuously perhaps at intervals between the close of the Thirty Years' War in 1648 and the coming of the Great Depression in 1929, the horizons seem to be wide open, and the varieties of good hope contending for allegiance are numerous. But the tidings of good hope don't become revolutionary except when the horizons begin to close in and the plausible versions of good hope have dwindled almost to the vanishing point.

For the kind of good hope that has the maximum historical impact is the one that capitalizes upon a prevalent despair at the corruption of the existing world, and then carries conviction in pointing to itself as the only possible exit from despair. Above everything else, revolutionaries are the men who keep their spirits up when everybody else's are sagging. In this sense, the greatest revolutionaries of the Western world to date have been precisely the early Christians who dared to affirm in the darkest days of the classical world that something far better was in process and could be salvaged from the ruins.

Both of these points are exemplified in the Biological Revolution that has now begun—despair at our present condition, but infinite hope for the future if the biologists' prescription is taken. Anybody looking for jeremiads on our present state could not do better than to consult the new biologists. "The facts of human reproduction," says Joshua Lederberg, "are all gloomy— the stratification of fecundity by economic status, the new environmental insults to our genes, the sheltering by humanitarian medicine of once-lethal genes."

More generally, the biologists deplore the aggressive instincts of the human animal, now armed with nuclear weapons, his lamentably low average intelligence for coping with increasingly complicated problems, and his terrible prolificity, no longer mitigated by a high enough death rate. It is precisely an aspect of the closing down of horizons and depletion of comfortable hopes in the second half of the twentieth century that conventional medicine is now seen by the biological revolutionaries as one of the greatest threats to the human race.

Yet mere prophets of gloom can never make a revolution. In fact, the new biologists are almost the only group among our contemporaries with a reasoned hopefulness about the long future—if the right path is taken. There are of course many individuals of a naturally cheerful or feckless temperament, today as always, but groups of men with an articulated hope for the future of the entire race are much rarer. The theologians no longer qualify, many Communists have lost their hold upon the future even by their own lights, and the only other serious contenders are the space scientists and astronauts. But just to get off the earth is a rather vague prescription for our ills. Few people even in the space program would make ambitious claims on this score. In a long historical retrospect, they may turn out to have been too modest.

This is not a charge that is likely ever to be leveled against the new biologists. It is well known by now that J. D. Watson begins his account of his double-helix double by saying that he had never seen Francis Crick in a modest mood. But after all, modesty is not the salient quality to be looked for in the new breed of biologists. If the world will only listen, they *know* how to put us on the high road to salvation.

Custom-made people

What exactly does their brand of salvation entail? Perhaps the most illuminating way to put the matter is that their ideal is the manufacture of man. In a manufacturing process, the number of units to be produced is a matter of rational calculation beforehand and of tight control thereafter. Within certain tolerances, specifications are laid down for a satisfactory product. Quality-control is maintained by checking the output and replacing defective parts. After the product has been put to use, spare parts can normally be supplied to replace those that have worn out.

This is the program of the new biologists—control of numbers by foolproof contraception; gene manipulation and substitution; surgical and biochemical intervention in the embryonic and neonatal phases; organ transplants or replacements at will.

Of these, only contraception is technically feasible at present. Routine organ transplants will probably be achieved for a wide range of suitable organs in less than five years. The grafting of mechanical organs, prosthetic devices inserted in the body, will probably take longer. Joshua Lederberg thinks that embryonic and neonatal intervention may be in flood tide by, say, 1984. As for gene manipulation and substitution in human beings, that is the remotest prospect of all— maybe by the year 2000. But we must not forget Lederberg's well-founded conviction that most predictions in these matters are likely to be too conservative. We are already five to ten years ahead of what most informed people expected to be the schedule for organ transplants in human beings.

The great question becomes, what is it going to be like to be living in a world where such things are coming true? How will the Biological Revolution affect our scheme of values? Nobody could possibly take in all the implications in advance, but some reasonable conjectures are in order.

It is virtually certain that the moral sanctions of birth control are going to be transformed. Down to the present time, the battle for birth control has been fought largely in terms of the individual couple's right to have the number of babies that they want at the desired intervals. But it is built into the quantity-controls envisioned by the Biological Revolution, the control of the biological inventory, that this is or ought to be a question of social policy rather than individual indulgence.

Many factors are converging upon many people to foster this general attitude, but the issue is particularly urgent from the point of view of the biological revolutionaries. In the measure that they succeed in making the human race healthier, first by transplants and later on by genetic tailoring, they will be inexorably swamped by their own successes unless world population is promptly brought under control. The irrepressible Malthus is springing from his lightly covered grave to threaten them with catastrophic victories.

Licensed babies

The only hope is birth control. The biologists can contribute the techniques, but the will to employ them on the requisite scale is another matter. The most startling proposal to date for actually enforcing birth control does not come from a biologist but from the Nobel-Prize-winning physicist W. B. Shockley, one of the inventors of the transistor. Shockley's plan is to render all women of childbearing age reversibly sterile by implanting a contraceptive capsule beneath the skin, to be removed by a physician only on the presentation of a government license to have a child. The mind boggles at the prospect of bootleg babies. This particular proposal is not likely to be enacted in the near future, even in India.

What we may reasonably expect is a continually rising chorus by the biologists, moralists, and social philosophers of the next generation to the effect that

nobody has a right to have children, and still less the
right to determine on personal grounds how many.
There are many reasons why a couple may not want to
be prolific anyhow, so that there might be a happy
coincidence between contraception seen by them as a
right and by statesmen and biologists as a duty. But the
suspicion is that even when people moderate their appetite in the matter of babies, they may still want to
have larger families than the earth can comfortably
support. The possibility of predetermining sex would
undoubtedly be helpful in this respect, but might not
be enough to make people forgo a third child. That is
where the conflict would arise between traditional
values, however moderately indulged, and the values
appropriate to the Biological Revolution.

This issue is bound to be fiercely debated. But
some of the most profound implications of the Biological Revolution may never present themselves for direct
ratification. In all probability, the issues will go by de-
fault as we gratefully accept specific boons from the
new biology.

Take, for example, the role of the patient in medicine. One of the principal strands in Western medicine
from the time of the Greeks has been the endeavor to
enlist the cooperation of the patient in his own cure.
In certain respects, this venerable tradition has grown
much stronger in the last century. Thus the rising incidence of degenerative diseases, like ulcers, heart trouble, and high blood pressure, has underscored the absolute necessity of inducing the patient to observe a
healthful regimen, literally a way of life.

This has been the whole point of Freudian psychiatry as a mode of therapy, that cures can be wrought
only by a painful exertion of the patient himself. We
often forget, for good reasons, how traditional Freud-

ianism is after the one big shock has been assimilated. In the present context, it actually epitomizes the Western tradition of bringing the patient's own personality to bear upon his medical problems.

Where do we go from here? The degenerative diseases are going to be dealt with increasingly by surgical repair of organs, by organ transplants, and later on by the installation of mechanical organs and eventually by the genetic deletion of weak organs before they occur. The incentive to curb your temper or watch your diet to keep your heart going will steadily decline.

As for mental illness, the near future almost certainly lies with psychopharmacology and the far future with genetic tailoring. Though the final pieces stubbornly decline to fall into place, the wise money is on the proposition that schizophrenia and other forms of psychosis are biochemical disorders susceptible of a pharmacological cure. If we are not presently curing any psychoses by drugs, we are tranquilizing and antidepressing many psychotics and emptying mental hospitals.

Neuroses, the theme of Freudian psychoanalysis, are another matter. It is not easy to envision a biochemical remedy for them. But even for neuroses, we already have forms of behavioral therapy that dispense with the Freudian tenet of implicating the patient in his own cure. For the *very* long future, it is certainly not inconceivable that genetic tailoring could delete neurotic propensities.

Everywhere we turn, the story is essentially the same. Cures are increasingly going to be wrought upon, done to, the patient as a passive object. The strength of his own personality, the force of his character, his capacity for reintegrating himself, are going to be increasingly irrelevant in medicine.

Genetic tailoring, boon or bane?

This leads to what many people would regard as
the biggest question of all. In what sense would we
have a self to integrate under the new dispensation?
The Princeton theologian Paul Ramsey has now been
appointed professor of "genetic ethics" at the George-
town University Medical School, presumably the first
appointment of its kind. He thinks that genetic tailoring would be a "violation of man." To this it must be
said that under the present scheme of things, many
babies get born with catastrophic genes that are not
exactly an enhancement of man. Our present genetic
self is a brute datum, sometimes very brutal, and anyhow it is hard to see how we can lose our identity before we have any.

As for installing new organs in the body, there is
no evident reason why the personality should be in-
fringed upon by heart or kidney transplants per se.
Brain transplants would be different, but surely they
would be among the last to come. States of mind regu-
lated by drugs we already possess, and obviously they
do alter our identity in greater or lesser degree. But
even here we must not forget that some identities are
intolerable to their distracted possessors.

We must not conclude, however, that the importance of these developments has been exaggerated.
The point is that the immediate practical consequences
will probably not present themselves as threatening to
the individuals involved—quite the contrary. Abstract
theological speculations about genetic tailoring would
be totally lost upon a woman who could be sure in
advance that her baby would not be born mentally retarded or physically handicapped. The private anxieties
of individuals are likely to diminish rather than increase

any effective resistance to the broader consequences of the Biological Revolution.

One of these is already implicit in predicting a sense of growing passivity on the part of patients, of not participating as a subject in their own recovery. This might well be matched by a more general sense of the inevitability of letting oneself be manipulated by technicians—of becoming an article of manufacture.

The difficulty becomes to estimate what psychological difference this would make. In any Hegelian overview of history, we can only become articles of manufacture because ''we'' have set up as the manufacturers. But the first person plural is a slippery customer. We the manufactured would be everybody and we the manufacturers a minority of scientists and technicians. Most people's capacity to identify with the satisfactions of the creative minority is certainly no greater in science than in other fields, and may well be less.

The beneficiaries of the Biological Revolution are not likely to feel that they are in control of the historical process from which they are benefiting. But they will not be able to indulge any feelings of alienation from science without endangering the specific benefits that they are unwilling to give up.

The best forecast would be for general acquiescence, though occasionally sullen, in whatever the Biological Revolution has to offer and gradually adjusting our values to signify that we approve of what we will actually be getting. The will to cooperate in being made biologically perfect is likely to take the place in the hierarchy of values that used to be occupied by being humbly submissive to spiritual counselors chastising the sinner for his own salvation. The new form of spiritual sloth will be not to want to be bodily perfect and genetically improved. The new avarice will be to cherish our miserable hoard of genes and favor the children that resemble us.

FURTHER THOUGHTS ON THE BIOLOGICAL REVOLUTION

READERS RESPONSE

Donald Fleming's article impresses me as a valid statement of the views of a strident biological minority, which would, if it could, impose a social and evolutionary disaster on man. The article ignores the early and needed applications of genetic engineering in (a) the alteration of micro-organisms as biological controls of pests and as more effective biochemical transformers —for example, of sewage into edible proteins; and (b) the modification of plants for desired properties.

Professor Fleming exaggerates the extent of today's genetic knowledge, especially with reference to metazoan species. Certainly, many genetic components are common throughout life, but it is equally clear that the aggregate quantity and organization of genetic information is vastly different in bacteria and man. This applies especially to the still obscure process of cellular differentiation (for example, why one cell becomes part of an eye rather than part of an intestine), and to polygenic traits (such as stature or components of intelligence), which are governed by the interactions of many gene loci.

More important, Fleming confuses the possibility of controlling specific traits with the maintenance of entire "desirable" types. The independent assortment of genes in sexual reproduction constantly introduces changes. The perfect replication of Superman is not possible; however, a "clone" of Superwomen might, in theory, be maintained through the asexual activation of eggs.

In general, Fleming's sources appear innocent of population genetics or modern evolutionary theory, as developed by Mayr, Dobzhansky, Hirsh, and others. In evolutionary perspective, man has been successful over a half-million years and through enormous change because of his variability and constant hybridization. Variability also has reduced conflict and promoted cooperation within the species—a fact well known for the basic variants: male and female. Characteristically, many of man's traits are at once "good" and "bad"; such worldwide diseases as juvenile diabetes and schizophrenia probably have highly desirable complements linked with energy mobilization and abstracting capacity. Moreover, man, as an old, successful species, carries a heavy burden of deleterious recessive genes which would be maintained by the close inbreeding needed to maintain specific traits. (Old frozen sperm, by the way, produces an increasing proportion of defective offspring.) All this means that genetic tinkering could produce many culls—how are they to be handled?

In any case, the introduction of tailormade man on any significant scale could only be done by the elimination of virtually all of today's social institutions and values. The development of the latter is, however, far more likely to achieve viable solutions to man's problems of survival and emotional satisfaction. Thus my prospective view for the year 2000 A.D. is not a Biological Dictatorship, but either a cultural collapse in the wake of nuclear war or a tamed biology ruled by more sophisticated Social Man.

(Demitri B. Shimkin
Professor of Anthropology and Geography
University of Illinois, Urbana, Illinois)

My own specialty is gerontology; and I am surprised Professor Fleming places as much stress as he does on organ transplant and says so little about the biochemical control of the aging process. I think that such control is implicit in modern molecular biology if understood and considered desirable.

Fleming's paper fails to make what I consider an important distinction. Extension of life-span past the age of frequent conception has a limited effect on the total population. While the extension of mature life-span is occurring, the proportion and number of older individuals do increase. However, the population is mainly determined by the rate of breeding and infant mortality. The population of the world is more dependent on the number of surviving great-grandchildren we produce than the length of our own lives. The world could well afford to have people live longer, as long as they were productive and provided that they did not contribute extra offspring.

Growing larger cerebral cortexes is not as sensational as suggested by Professor Fleming. We have discussed the matter a number of times in our own laboratory, and I am sure that somewhere experiments are under way. The questions are technical—what agents should be used, would they cross the placenta, how would they affect uterine blood flow, and what other effects would there be on the developing embryo?

I believe Professor Fleming misses one point, and that is that before genetic tampering becomes commonplace, there is going to be a period where people will have a good deal of latitude in determining the causes of their death and the risk they will run with particular diseases. Many situations will arise where a course of action might result in less probability of cardiovascular disease and more probability of cancer. The person who receives a transplant runs more risk from infectious disease. I am sure that there will be a risk concerned with gene manipulation of the type that is being discussed in this article. Efforts to introduce more perfect genetic information will always run a risk of damaging other genetic information. The patient, instead of making no decisions, may face the problem of making a good many more. I don't really believe that the biological revolution is a threat to the individual. I would hope that he could aspire to a more creative, better life and that he would have more time for his education, a successful career, and the enjoyable use of his leisure time.

(F. Marott Sinex
Chairman, Department of Biochemistry
Boston University School of Medicine
Boston, Massachusetts)

Most of the promises of the New Biology enumerated by Professor Fleming will doubtless be fulfilled sooner or later. But these promises are really of two quite different categories. Some will alleviate human suffering without endeavoring to change the basic nature of human beings; others purport to create new kinds of beings by altering their genetic composition.

The biologists, unfortunately, are generally so preoccupied with the genetically determined instinctive characteristics of man as an animal that they tend to ignore the role of cultural activities in human affairs.

Culture, not inheritance, sets the values of different societies. Generally speaking, changes within the societies
of *Homo sapiens* will be accomplished with varying de-
grees of difficulty, and social science analysis can pre-
dict the acceptability of such changes within limits.
Genetic alteration of *Homo sapiens* into another species,
however, involves problems of qualitative transformations, which leads into the unknown.

The late Hermann Muller, Nobel laureate in genetics, whom Professor Fleming cites with approval,
proposed a sperm bank to select people who are genetically more healthy, intelligent, and cooperative.
Professor Fleming seems to believe that someday gene
manipulation can remove the "aggressive instincts of
the human animal" and increase "his lamentably low
average intelligence for coping with increasingly complicated problems." Others have discussed man's instinct for territoriality and his aggressiveness in defense of his habitat, and some primatologists attempt
to trace the roots of human society to vague instincts
shared with primate ancestors and the whole animal
kingdom.

The most elementary knowledge of the history of
culture and of its varieties should make it clear to anyone that man is cooperative or aggressive, territorial or
nonterritorial, warring or peaceful according to cultural circumstances, and that only the emotional components of these varieties of behavior arise from the
basic qualities of all human beings. At present, therefore, it is more realistic to think of how culture can be
changed than how man may be altered to respond
instinctively to a culture not yet envisaged.

The most alarming ethical aspect of the proposed
use of the New Biology is that the nature of the genetic
transformations shall be stipulated by those of superior
intelligence, and that the remainder of the population
shall conform to the needs of society, childbearing

being licensed. Not only is it unlikely that specific temperaments and forms of behavior that are socially desirable have any genetic basis, but intelligence alone by no means assures an answer to social problems.

One has only to think of the intellectual eminence of the Nobel laureates in their own fields as compared with their basic misunderstanding of the implications of the proposals discussed here. No one will object to intelligence per se, but it is by no means a simple Mendelian factor. Moreover, it becomes effective only when trained and applied to specific problems by means of an appropriate methodology. Such efforts have scarcely begun.

To entrust the remodeling of the basic nature of *Homo sapiens* into a new species, with more clearly conceived characteristics than docility in the hands of their masters, will rightly be opposed. If use of drugs and chemicals, surgery, electrodes in the brain, brainwashing, and other techniques are added, I can only picture a new race of zombies, and it occurs to me that mechanical robots would be cheaper and better behaved.

At a moment in history when nonwhite races are striving for self-identification and dignity, it is deeply disturbing that the old eugenics should be offered with pseudoscientific claims. Not all the New Biologists have any such goals, and one must hope that they would refuse to be part of the intellectual caste of dictators. One thing is clear about our present society: the required freedom of research which makes the New Biology possible will also make individuals rebel against such a new society.

(Julian H. Steward
Professor of Anthropology,
University of Illinois,
Urbana, Illinois)

The claim that molecular and organismic biology no longer "constitute a community" is sheer rubbish. And rubbish it would remain even if some Nobel Prize winner endorsed it. The great discoveries which enriched biology in recent years have given biology, the science of life, an unmistakable coherence, not a schizophrenia. Life has two aspects, equally significant and equally fascinating—its unity and its diversity. It is purblindness or puerility to ignore either.

Yes indeed, we may be entering a century of biology. Yes indeed, it would be a bold man who would deny that the possibilities outlined in Mr. Fleming's article may someday be realized. It takes an even bolder, or perhaps a thoughtless, man to be sure that they will be realized by the year 2000. And when and if they will, biologists had better keep in mind that the application of these and other possible discoveries to man will raise a host of tough problems, which will be sociological, ethical, and even political, rather than primarily biological, in nature.

(Theodosius Dobzhansky
The Rockefeller University
New York, New York)

Professor Fleming's article is encouraging in that it indicates scientists are becoming concerned with the social consequences of their discoveries. However, it is difficult to see how the technological discoveries he lists can be described as a "revolution." Indeed, many of them are little more than faint hopes or biological curiosities, and one of them, the preconceptual determination of sex, is no closer to solution now than it has been for the past thirty or forty years. To put these matters into proper perspective, the major unsolved practical problems of today are those of poverty, violence, warfare, overpopulation, and last but not least, a general rising tide of discontent with a bureaucratic and impersonally organized society.

These are social and ecological problems, and their solution is most likely to come from the efforts of scientists in the behavioral sciences and the ecological portion of biological science. Indeed, there are two centers of ferment and discovery in the biological sciences at the present time, located at almost opposite poles of complexity of organization. One of these is molecular biology as described by Professor Fleming, arising from the application of new biochemical techniques to basic biological processes. The other is animal behavior, including the study of animal societies and their ecology. While the nature of the social problems is so complex that they will require the best efforts of all sorts of sciences for their solution, it is from the latter area of biology rather than the former that possible solutions of our major problems are most likely to come.

For example, the population problem is likely to be augmented rather than diminished as constitutional diseases are cured and embryos are provided a better prenatal environment. While the newer methods of contraception are somewhat more convenient than the old, the way in which these techniques may be used to bring about a desirable result provides an extraordinarily complex problem of social control and social engineering. We still have too many narrowly trained scientists who anticipate that all human ills will be removed by one simple technical discovery, and each hopes that that discovery will come from his own discipline. What we need is a new breed of scientists who are aware of the complex and interdependent nature of biological and social processes, and who have the ability and motivation to cooperate with each other in attempting to understand and control these processes.

(J. P. Scott
Director, Center for Research on
Social Behavior
Bowling Green State University
Bowling Green, Ohio)

I see no excuse for beefing up brains. The human range of neurons in excess over basic mammalian needs ranges from 7 to 12 billion, almost 2 to 1. We don't need more than 12 million, only more people with better prefrontal areas and thus better judgment. A computer is a better storage house for excess information than a top-heavy skull.

If all these biological breakthroughs were employed, death might be abolished, and if it were, cultural change would be too. A frozen status quo is itself death, the end of the world, as presented by the Harvard *Lampoon* in its parody of *Life* in October, 1968.

But who is going to persuade or force people to accept these changes? Must we have a tighter dictatorship than any that the world has yet seen, or a reign of terror controlled by a Nobel laureate in a spaceship? Before it is too late, it might be wise to abolish the Nobel Prize as the world's greatest breeder of arrogance. Statements like "We will succeed in doing such and such by A.D. 1985," or "A.D. 2000," etc. remind me of the Arab story of the little men underground trying to dig their way out to daylight and destroy the world. Every night they say, "Tomorrow we will break through," but God fills in their holes because they forgot to say *Inshallah* (God willing). Perhaps these superbiologists might find some way to say their equivalent of *Inshallah*, or to cross their fingers when they set their timetables.

(Carleton S. Coon
Gloucester, Massachusetts)

The revolution that Dr. Fleming describes is real enough, but I do not feel that he has really come to grips with its implications. I kept asking myself "So what?" at each new revelation, and it is a good question. What Fleming fails to do—yet he is certainly equipped to do it—is to spell out what the biological engineering he describes will do to the traditional structure of American society. How, specifically, will it affect our egalitarian ideals, our laws, our lives? He hints at some of the answers—for example, the relief that might be felt by many adults if they could justify *not* having children—but such hints are not enough. Fleming, it seems to me, treats his "revolutionaries" entirely too gently. He is in awe of them and handles them with kid gloves. I would much prefer a bolder attack.

Joshua Lederberg may be a genius with macromolecules, but he would appear to be a rather untrustworthy kind of guide to the new, biologically engineered society. What are his qualifications for this task? What are the implications of publicly sponsored research being used to destroy the institutions of the society paying for the research? How much autonomy should be granted scientists when the results of their research have implications of fundamental importance to society? These are questions that desperately need answers today; unfortunately, Fleming does not even raise them. I wish he had.

(L. Pearce Williams
Professor of the History of Science
Cornell University, Ithaca, New York)

I believe that Donald Fleming has quite misconstrued or at best oversimplified my own position on the subject he discusses.

I am indeed fascinated by embryology, since so much of the biochemical and physiological machinery of the body is laid down during fetal life. But I am equally fascinated by the psychological and social development of the child afterward. I would take particular exception to the phrase "maddened and obsessed," unless it is answered that my concern for healthy maternal nutrition to sustain the fetus' developing brain is an obsession. I think the further phrase "such a waste of time before the scientists can get at us" is particularly offensive—if Mr. Fleming wants to voice such an opinion on his own account, that is fine with me, but I hate to have even an indirect attribution of such language to myself appearing on the record. I also have to stress that the emphasis I have given to "euphenics" is a counterslogan in reaction to the zealous eugenicists. I pointed out elsewhere that euphenics is in fact nothing but medicine.

Mr. Fleming has certainly misunderstood me if he believes that I advocate a program of action. I do advocate that research that can enable us to achieve the human mastery of nature that has been the main thread of his cultural development; and I advocate the widest possible public education about these opportunities precisely in order to minimize the chance that they will be dominated by monolithic bureaucracy. For example, I am quite opposed to "foolproof compulsory contraception." At the same time, I join a great many biologists and others in warning that we must somehow achieve a humane solution to the very pressing problem of world overpopulation and underdevelopment.

As to organ replacements, I was among the first to point out the difficulties that would arise in managing the potential "market" in organs, and primarily for that reason, pointed out the need to stress some countertechnology in the direction of artificial organs.

I do not see any prospect of gene manipulation and substitution along the lines specifically laid out by

Fleming, but I certainly do see new possibilities of therapeutic repair of those diseases about which we achieve sufficient biochemical understanding.

I do favor continued research on human development, particularly on the correlated questions of the development of the brain and of intellect, and there is no doubt that such research will provide answers to many tragic questions that plague people today.

I am in accord with Mr. Fleming in his cautions that the opportunities for more and more incisive intervention may have cumulatively insidious by-products, and that these will be far the worse if we do not broaden the base of public understanding of biology.

Finally, let me state one specific program that I do advocate and a theme to which I have returned again and again in my columns. The world's most pressing problems are the nutrition and education of the young.

(Joshua Lederberg
Professor of Genetics
Stanford University School of Medicine
Palo Alto, California)

It is too bad that Professor Fleming emphasizes the split at Harvard between the "old" and "new" biologies. Harvard in this area is way behind the times, and now appears to be going through the sort of convulsions which characterized other departments nearly a decade ago (and which Stanford was very fortunate to avoid). It is now abundantly clear that biologists of all persuasions must remain in close touch while attempting to solve the fantastic problems now confronting mankind. Many molecular biologists, presumably because of their extremely narrow training, have promoted preposterous systems of priority in biological research. One need only consider the money which over the past decades has flowed into what broadly can be described as "cancer research" in contrast to what has gone into research in areas related to population control. Cancer is a disease primarily of concern to older people in a world where almost 40 percent of the people are under fifteen years of age. The population explosion threatens to exterminate us all. On the other hand, "classical biologists," out of envy, ignorance, or stupidity, have all too often denigrated the striking advances made in molecular biology, refused to see their importance in all biological disciplines, and have reacted too defensively against the molecular biologists. The time has long since passed for this kind of nonsense. The brilliance of the molecular biologist must be directed first at problems of immediate importance, and the classical biologists must bring more rigor to bear on those problems which are too complex for a simple chemical solution.

If we had the time, perhaps the most interesting study of all would be essentially the study of the theology of science. There already has been one immensely interesting contribution to this area in Professor James Watson's superb book *The Double Helix*. Scientists could profitably spend more time trying to understand their own motives and faiths rather than promoting the corny ideas of how science operates that are characteristically repeated to secondary school students.

(Paul R. Ehrlich
Professor of Biology, Stanford University
Stanford, California)

Dr. Fleming's review of the revolutionary implications of some of the recent discoveries in biological science is challenging, even if there will be some disagreement as to the equal validity or equal importance of each of his twelve items.

The omissions seem to me to be the more important. Decisions will have to be made about whether

and how to use our increasing ability to control hitherto
uncontrollable natural and biological processes. These
decisions will have great individual and sociological
importance; and in addition, they are emotionally
highly charged. Therefore they require men who are
both erudite and emotionally mature. But to produce
this combination in abundance implies revolutionary
developments in the educational process. This cannot
even begin until we acknowledge the fact that in the
entire history of human culture, erudition and wisdom
have had at most a purely accidental correlation.

I agree wholly that we must accept the responsibility of bringing order into planning the intervals and
gender sequences of family life. Among the thousands
of other variables which determine the processes of
growth in human life, these have special and early importance. Once we have this knowledge, however, we
will face the problem of how to use it. I agree that the
right to prevent conception or to interrupt it will soon
be taken for granted, and that our main problem will
then be to determine how to induce people to use these
rights. In itself this is an unsolved psychological and
psychosocial problem on conscious, preconscious, and
unconscious levels.

Even more fundamental will be the next problem
—namely, to ascertain who has a right to have babies
at all, and when, and how frequently, and at what intervals. So I agree that we will have to consider every
possible technique by which genetic determinants can
be ascertained, selected, and brought into harmonious
use and control. But this implies again the same revolution in education, because to determine what are the
most favorable intervals and the most favorable gender
sequences in any family unit demands a special kind
and degree of maturity.

Finally, as we attempt this, we will also have to
avoid the danger of reverting to the ancient fallacy that

genetics can operate in a vacuum. There is some danger that Professor Fleming's thesis, if accepted uncritically, will throw us back to a modern version of the ancient and unreal controversy between heredity and environment, as though either ever operates apart from the other.

For example, recent studies of infants have shown that in addition to genetic factors, inadequate nutrition can block the development of brain size, of the central nervous system as a whole, and of the IQ. But "nutrition" involves emotional as well as caloric and biochemical ingredients. So genetic factors do not operate independent of nutritional and other factors, and to select genetic factors for separate and isolated emphasis brings a danger of overlooking other concurrent determinants.

Professor Fleming steps furthest from his own field when he discusses drugs and the brain. In principle there is nothing new about the so-called hallucinogens and their simulation of psychotic states. Alcohol was doing this long before anyone coined the term "psychopharmacology." The fact that such deliria are a form of psychosis does not lead to the unwarranted conclusion that psychosis is due to some inborn error of metabolism which is remediable by the administration of drugs. This is an unwarranted assumption made by Linus Pauling and others who have observed this field only from clinically naïve armchairs. Even if true, the existence of a drug delirium does not prove this thesis, whether the drug is alcohol or LSD. We must not assume too much that is still unknown about the relation of the hallucinogens to the psychotic disorganization of the neurotic process.

Similarly, the lack of a tranquilizer is not the *cause* of a psychosis any more than a lack of aspirin is a *cause* of headaches. Actually, it is not always clear when a drug is therapeutic in any real sense, or when it simply masks symptoms to produce a temporary illusion of health while the underlying process of illness goes on unimpeded until even greater disorganization occurs. Also, when drugs make an illness accessible to psychotherapy, this is a valuable achievement, but only when the opportunity is seized upon by experienced psychotherapists. I am unhappy to see the current newspaper ballyhoo over psychopharmacology and hallucinogens given such unwarranted support.

(Lawrence S. Kubie
Sparks, Maryland)

I consider it improbable, not impossible, that within this century eugenics by biological engineering will become feasible for man; that "euphenics" will become a reality; that it will be possible to prevent and cure mental diseases by drugs, although they will be increasingly important in ameliorating symptoms; or that the transplantation of organs will become more than an act of desperation to gain a worthwhile prolongation of life.

It is my opinion that the processes of life and development are too complex to be mastered to the extent predicted by Professor Fleming.

It is my opinion that predictions of successful transplantation of the human brain require gross ignorance or disregard for the complexity of its anatomical connections. Prolonged survival of the *caput* without a body is more probable.

(Dwight J. Ingle
Editor, Perspectives in Biology
and Medicine
Chicago, Illinois)

ABORTION IS NOT THE ANSWER

BY EUNICE KENNEDY SHRIVER

Should a woman be forced to bear within her body the product of a rape? The body of a deformed fetus?

Should the poverty of the poor be increased by the burden of "too many children"?

Should hundreds of thousands of "unwanted" children be annually imposed on parents and on society?

Shouldn't abortion laws be "liberalized" to deal with these problems? Shouldn't abortion be made easier? Should it not be a second line of defense when contraception fails?

George Gallup and Louis Harris—if they asked these questions in this way—would very likely discover that most Americans, regardless of religion, agree on the answers.

Eunice Shriver, sister of the late President Kennedy, is married to R. Sargent Shriver, present United States Ambassador to France.

"Abortion is Not the Answer" first appeared in McCall's magazine (April, 1968) and is reprinted here through the courtesy of the author.

Except for country-club memberships, Americans do *not* favor restrictions on anything, even on speeding. And they certainly do not favor too many children or unwanted children or rape or deformed children or poverty.

Advocates of changes in the abortion law today are riding the wave of this permissive, libertarian, individualistic temper of our times. There is little doubt that they will win their way—that many existing restraints on abortion will be eliminated from our laws. It has already happened in some states; the process is well under way in others.

Given this situation, is there anything useful to be said? My answer is yes. I think there is much that needs to be said before sincere men and women can reach socially responsible conclusions to this debate. I do not approve of using the criminal code to impose my personal moral standards—or anyone else's—on the whole of society. Nor am I indifferent to the personal suffering and social costs represented by unwanted pregnancies. On the contrary, it was because of my concern for what is happening to so many children in our country, especially to handicapped or defective children, that I have devoted a large part of my time for fifteen years to the problems of the mentally retarded. Abortion is part of this picture. I am convinced that mere changes in the abortion laws constitute a terribly inadequate response to the conditions that motivate the advocates for reform. I believe that mere legal reform may even add to human anguish and social decay, that it evades the core problems instead of solving them—or that, at best, it treats symptoms rather than the underlying conditions.

To anyone who thinks about this issue for even five minutes, it will be obvious that the demand for easier abortion can hardly be a spontaneous, natural phenomenon. Abortion is an unpleasant subject to discuss, a distasteful operation for doctors to perform, a wretched experience for women to undergo. And no one will ever persuade me that the mothers of today suddenly are strangely indifferent to the new life present within them when they conceive a child.

That is why I say the rising incidence of abortion is only a symptom. Abortion points to deeper personal problems, problems often rooted in profound social disorders. When race riots explode in our cities, we know that merely repressing them will not get at their causes. So, also, when hundreds of thousands of women experience pregnancy not as a blessing but as an intolerable threat, it does not follow that their true needs will be met just by making it easier for them to empty their wombs.

The strength of the case for legal change is the fact—which nobody denies—that for many women today pregnancy may create heartbreaking dilemmas or impose burdens beyond their capacity. The reformers cite pregnancy caused by rape or incest, or those that may result in a defective child or that can be said to threaten the mental or physical health of the mother, and they urge that situations like these be recognized as grounds for legal abortion. More extreme reformers point out that these dramatic cases comprise only a small fraction of the illegal abortions now being performed; their conclusion is that we should grant abortion on request.

If only to legalize what is now happening in hospitals and doctors' offices, it is quite likely that more of our states will amend their abortion laws to one extent or another. Before we argue whether this answer to the problem is the one most in accord with our highest ethical standards, I want to ask whether legal reform is a *sufficient* answer? Is it the best we can do? Now that we recognize the dimensions of the problems facing mothers and children and the anguish confronting them, is our society capable of no better response than an amendment of our criminal codes?

If I may echo a phrase constantly voiced by my brother, the late President, I think we can do better. Instead of being content with legalistic tinkering, I would urgently propose that we try to change the conditions that cause people to seek abortion. We should not address ourselves only to the scab, when it is possible—not easy, but possible—to get at the causes, to put some medicine where the pain originates.

I certainly agree that tolerance is a good thing— when it is applied to people. But I think we should be *intolerant* toward anything that makes it difficult for a woman who has conceived a child to bring him into the world in joy and gladness—confident that if some problems rise that are beyond her capacity, she can trust her community, like a larger family surrounding and supporting her, to provide the assistance she needs. We speak so glibly of "unwanted" children and of the problems they create or become, and we seem to be turning all too readily to a solution that will simply eliminate them before they emerge into our midst.

Why not ask, instead, *why* they are unwanted? It is often because of conditions that could be changed if we only had the will. Then, too, today we know that no woman need have unplanned pregnancies. Why multiply abortions—at best, a negative, destructive solution—when we have not begun to do enough to make birth control universally understood, universally available to anyone who truly needs it?

It may be that the attitude I am recommending will not be persuasive unless exemplified in concrete detail. In that spirit, I offer the following proposals, acknowledging in advance that not all are equally important or equally easy to carry out and that all would benefit from the refining process of legislative hearings.

Counseling: Even if we think that legal abortion

is sometimes permissible, is the mere granting of permission an adequate response from the community? I cannot believe so. A woman who requests an abortion is acting to meet a crisis in her life—and she may be acting out of fear and in a state of high tension, oblivious to other possible solutions. If abortion reform is guided by true compassion and wisdom, it will include provision for psychiatric, psychological, religious, and legal advice, available immediately to any woman who asks to be aborted. Such service should *not* be offered timidly, hesitantly. And it should not be remote from the hospital or other authorized location for therapeutic abortion. It should be intrinsic to the process of "legalized abortion," and it should be required where a cooling-off period is possible before any abortion is necessary.

Involvement of Fathers: In any abortion, at least half the problem is the father. Therefore, if there is a lawful father, I propose that he be joined in the counseling process, that his responsibility be as fully examined and explained as the mother's, and that he be required to agree with the proposed abortion. Why should the woman alone bear the possible burden of self-recrimination, guilt, or second-guessing, while the man goes scot-free? Why not utilize whatever strength he may be able to contribute? Why not acknowledge the rights he may justly claim in a given situation? And if the mother is a teen-age, unmarried girl, what about her parents and her boy friend? Should not their share of responsibility be recognized and their help elicited?

Birth Insurance: Thousands of devoted mothers and fathers have proved that the birth of a defective child need not be pure tragedy; often such a child becomes a focal point of family love. Eighty-five percent of the retarded can get jobs and adjust to society. They give love and receive it—and who will say they ought not to have lived at all?

Yet in some cases a defective child imposes enormous economic burdens on the parents. Why is it, I wonder, that we have never seriously investigated the possibility of "birth insurance," to protect families against such eventualities, either through private companies backed by government or through some such agency as Social Security? Then every family would have the means to see to it that their baby had proper care and attention, either at home or, when advisable, in a well-run institution, and other children in the family would not be deprived of educational and other advantages because of their handicapped brother or sister.

Let me pause to contrast this situation with that of abortion reform. Except in a small number of cases, the chances of accurately predicting abnormality in a given fetus are not more than one in four; and even when there is abnormality, no one can tell in advance how serious the abnormality will be. When we legalize abortion on this ground, it means that three normal fetuses will be "terminated" for the sake of eliminating one abnormal one. This seems to me a cruel form of Russian roulette.

Which speaks better for us as human beings and as a humane civilization—to provide special help for the weakest, most defenseless among us or to authorize their extinction? I think the answer is beyond debate.

Vaccination: This same contrast in values shows up in other ways. For example, if we are greatly concerned about mental retardation in children, there is something we can do about it right now—for we already have vaccines to prevent the occurrence of common measles, a cause of retardation.

In 1966, the experts estimate that there were more than 600,000 cases of common measles in this country that left 200 children between the ages of one and 12 dead and an additional 400 mentally retarded.

Today there are still 6,000,000 children who have not been vaccinated.

However, if a pregnant woman contracts German measles during the early weeks of pregnancy, the chances are better than two to one that her child will suffer some form of physical or mental impairment. A new German-measles vaccine is now being tested and is expected to be approved within the next eighteen months—long before the next expected epidemic. When it becomes available, every state should require all girls who are not naturally immunized to receive this vaccination before they reach childbearing age.

"Unwanted" Babies: Many babies are unwanted not because their parents are selfish but because they are realistic; they know, with bitter certainty, the kind of life they can offer the child and the effect on the rest of the family of another mouth to feed, another body to clothe.

Mrs. Dorothy Height, president of the National Council of Negro Women, has put it bluntly: "It isn't just the woman who decides whether her child is unwanted. Society has put a label on who is unwanted. But it has not taken the responsibility for developing equal conditions of life, in which that child *can* be wanted."

Our government is making some effort in this direction, in the form of Head Start classes, job training, parent-and-child centers. Private business and labor unions are accepting greater responsibility for opening jobs and training men to hold them. But these programs need to be multiplied in scope—and sadly the mood of much of America is to reduce, not extend such efforts.

Most importantly, we should consider a family-allowance plan, under which the head of each family receives a certain amount of money per child each month. Some commentators say this is visionary and that it will not make a vital difference in the lives of families.

Yet the United States is *the only industrial democracy in the world* that does not have such a plan. We have only to look to Canada to learn that such a program can be both economically sound and socially effective.

Even if we go the whole route and accept abortion on demand, we will not begin to solve the problem of unwanted children—and even if we could, it would not be the most responsible and humane solution. If we reject such solutions as the family-allowance plan, we will condemn another generation of parents to despair, and their children to neglect or to death before birth—which is another name for abortion.

Education for Responsible Parenthood: Nearly every state requires physical-fitness classes in our public schools, to assure a strong and healthy citizenry. Many states require driver-training classes, to help prevent accidents. Yet courses in marriage and parenthood are not nearly so universal; we let our young people embark on matrimony with very little idea of what they are doing. Nearly any girl can bear a baby, nearly every boy can beget a child; but it takes more than sex to be a successful mother or father, to find fulfillment in parenthood, to meet its responsibilities.

I believe that parenthood courses—with full scholastic credits—(I am not referring to the sex-instruction courses now being offered in some schools) should be provided for every high-school student in this country. In addition to lectures on infant and child development, both boys and girls should work with the very young in Head Start, kindergarten, and nursery-school programs—observing, caring for, playing with infants and small children, seeing their mental as well as physical growth. How many teen-agers know that praising a two-year-old's good acts will make him more eager to learn at five? How many know that speaking and singing to a child of nine months increases his vocabulary and IQ? How many young parents understand that a child's talents can be permanently awakened—or repressed—before age six?

If we want to "do something about abortion," we ought to do something about parenthood. Fully 80 percent of the abortions performed annually in this country have nothing to do with rape, incest, illegitimacy, defective fetuses, or physical or mental health. If we are looking for the causes of these abortions, we surely must include on the list a widespread failure to appreciate either the responsibilities or the pleasures of parenthood.

Defenders of the Fetus: Who will speak for the unborn baby? Modern science reveals that the fetus—even at four weeks—has a functioning, beating heart. And by eight weeks, the fetus has a central nervous system; well-developed muscles and nerves; an ingestive, digestive, and excretory system; an identifiable cranium, with brain cells; ears, eyes, nose, toes, fingers, arms, and even sweat glands. He can move his head and bend his body; he is even sensitive to touch.

But one thing the fetus cannot do is plead his own cause before the human race, of which he is so clearly a member. And since he cannot speak, should anyone speak for him? I believe so. Our common and statutory law cannot acknowledge the presence of a soul; but if the law is going to reflect the scientific reality, it should at least recognize that the fetus is a unique creature with an awesome potential.

Unfortunately, the reforms now being urged on us offer nothing in this direction. Those who urge abortion on request leave the decision entirely to the mother. Yet she did not conceive the child alone, and she is not alone in the universe. The proposals submitted by more moderate reformers usually entrust the decision to a panel of doctors. But abortion is not solely a medical question, and treating it as such denies the interest of society in the fetus, the mother, and the family. I propose, therefore, that all legal abortions be approved not just by two or three physicians but also by a layman, preferably an attorney, who would be required to state that he had personally brought the rights of the fetus to the attention of the doctors and parents.

Mental Health: A threat to mental health rising from pregnancy has become one of the leading arguments to justify an abortion—and in some cases it can, indeed, be a tragic and compelling reason. Yet psychologists themselves say that genuine cases of mental sickness arising from pregnancy are rare. Most women who go to them asking for an abortion on mental-health grounds are not suffering from any specific mental disease; the realistic truth is that they want an abortion to enhance or preserve their own comfort.

If mental health is to be a legal justification for abortion, I think it must be defined strictly and that the best efforts of legislators and doctors should unite to find criteria of mental health that can be interpreted with reasonable uniformity. Otherwise, the very term may become a joke, and psychiatry itself may be open to derision. This is not a possibility to be taken lightly by the profession or by the public it serves.

Illegitimacy: About 20 percent of the women who have abortions in the United States are unmarried. Some are divorced women, but most are young girls "in trouble." The latter often suffer from psychological problems that abortion cannot cure, and without some form of counseling, they will almost inevitably become pregnant again. Others are girls who discover after pregnancy that the love affair is not encompassing enough to include a child.

Such girls do not choose abortion for its own sake, any more than any other woman would, but rather as an alternative to social ostracism or forced marriage. The approach I am urging suggests that we should do something about these factors, instead of punishing the unborn child for the mistake of his mother and father. We need not approve premarital sex, whether casual or intense, to lighten the pressure of disapproval that makes abortion seem a lesser evil. But we can cease being hysterical and hypocritical about it. And we can multiply the number of agencies like the Florence Crittenden Homes for unwed mothers, where girls can go for the last five months of pregnancy, where they can continue their studies, get help with emotional problems, find guidance for the future.

Despite the wide variety of programs I have described, I believe there is a kind of unity that binds them. What I want most urgently to convey is not the details of the programs, but the approach, which I believe can be extended to every aspect of the abortion problem. Abortion need not be the wave of the future. There are other solutions I think are preferable—not because they are quicker and easier, but because they show more respect for human beings as they really are, for the sexual act in all its implications, for parenthood, and for community.

I have found support for this approach in the spoken and written thought of Protestant, Jewish, and Catholic ethics and in the reflections of agnostic physicians, scientists, and humanists. This evidence became abundantly clear at a recent international conference on abortion, at which 73 experts—lawyers, doctors, public officials, social scientists, clergymen of all faiths—discussed abortion from every possible viewpoint.

The conferees raised familiar unsolved questions —and others I have never dreamed of. Is a human fetus the full equivalent of human life, or just a part of the mother's body tissue? Should a woman have unrestricted autonomy over her own body? Or do her husband, her children, her society, her God have lawful interests, too? Will we tolerate imperfections in human beings? If not, how will we draw the line between those who will live and those who will die? And who will draw the line? What kind of family do we want? What kind of society will we become?

Among the remarks that impressed me most at the conference was a simple but unexpected comparison offered by Dr. Robert E. Cooke, chief of pediatrics at Johns Hopkins Hospital. He invited us to look at abortion in relation to a tonsillectomy—which, like abortion, is regarded by doctors as neither difficult nor particularly dangerous—and then to reflect on the difference in the way society regards the two operations.

Both operations involve the removal of tissue. Both tissues are alive; both are composed of chemical compounds, DNA and RNA molecules. Their physical structure may vary slightly, but basically both are globs of matter composed of cells, which, in turn, are composed of chemicals. Where is the difference?

First, a given sample of fetal tissue is unique: There never was and never will be another piece of tissue identical to it. In contrast, the tonsil tissue removed is closely related to all the other tissue in the same person's body.

Second, fetal tissue is different from the parent organism. The chromosome composition of fetal tissue, its genetic makeup, is fixed at conception and differs from that of the parents—from the mother's quite as much as from the father's. Your tonsils are yours and yours alone, but the fetal tissue within a woman's body is not hers, though she nourishes it. Which raises the interesting question: Whose is it?

But it is the third difference, the *potential* of the human fetal tissue, that concerns us. Unless molested, human fetal tissue has the capability of developing into an individual like ourselves, to be like us, to be in our image, to be human.

Perhaps the reason I am struck by this comparison is that arguments favoring abortion generally proceed on the assumption that life outside the womb is somehow essentially distinct from life within the womb. In opposition to this theory are recent discoveries in genetics, showing that the genetic potential which directs the development of all human life is fully established at the moment of conception, when the mother's egg is fertilized by the father's sperm. Once that egg is implanted in the womb, no new genetic matter is ever added.

I believe that God is our creator, that He made us to his own image and likeness, that He is the steward of our life, and that He has not granted us power over other innocent lives. For everything we know of God tells us that He values the life of every human being and commands us to respect and safeguard it at every stage, in every condition and circumstance. Having sure knowledge of the uniqueness and potential of the life within a mother's womb, I cannot grasp how we can righteously claim authority to destroy it.

In saying these things, of course, I speak from faith—not because I expect all others to share my beliefs, but because I believe the choice of abortion as the solution for social problems has very deep implications for our future.

Today, the magazines young girls read, the television programs women watch, the advertising they see, all glorify sex or exploit it. The pill and other methods of birth control offer the shimmering possibility of sex without pregnancy; sex for fun and gratification; sex without any need for the deep sense of personal responsibility for one's sexual acts that once was fostered by the ever-present possibility of generating new life.

Increasingly, our society accepts divorce, premarital relations, and extramarital relations as prerogatives of the "liberated woman"—and now abortion allows women to extend yet further the range of their freedom.

In my judgment, such abuses can create a dangerous drift into what I would call the "Hard Society." I would define the Hard Society as one without love—where everyone takes care of himself, where people use one another to satisfy their desires, but do not get involved with one another, because they do not want the responsibilities that go with permanent or deep relationships.

Every woman contemplates her *first* abortion with misgivings; she senses that she is participating in the killing of "something." Though some continue to experience guilt, for others this feeling is soon overcome by a sense of relief that it is over. The second and third abortions pose fewer moral questions, raise fewer, if any, qualms. Abortion has hardened such a woman and, in so doing, has helped harden society.

But the Hard Society is more than easy sex and widespread, easy abortion. It is a society characterized by separateness between rich and poor, between whites and blacks, between an intellectual elite and the unlearned masses, where both individuals and blocs are concerned solely with maximizing their own comforts and enforcing their own prejudices.

Love is the true enemy of the Hard Society—and love is the most needed ingredient in solving the problems of abortion. If we are moved by love and not by expediency, I believe we will respond to the conditions that favor abortion in the ways I have tried to suggest, and in other ways, as well. There is no question that the people of the richest country in history can afford the cost of these proposals. The question is, rather, whether our values are firm enough, our compassion strong enough to undertake this quest.

Instead of becoming the Hard Society, we could become a just and compassionate one. Instead of destroying life, we could destroy the conditions that make life intolerable. In this society, every child, regardless of his capacities or the circumstances of his birth, would be welcomed, loved, and cared for—and abortion would cease to preoccupy us, because it would not be necessary.

This would be a great blessing, but not the only one. For, as Teilhard de Chardin has written, "Some day, after mastering the winds, the waves, the tides and gravity, we shall harness for God the energies of love, and then, for the second time in the history of the world, man will discover fire."

LIBERALIZE ABORTION LAWS

BY DR. ALAN F. GUTTMACHER

Five years ago, during the depths of the thalidomide horror, in which a supposedly harmless drug produced deformed babies, my telephone rang in the middle of the night. "Dr. Guttmacher, this is the 'New York Daily News.' Will you abort Sherri Finkbine? The fee is of no importance." Half asleep, I reacted with the expletive "Hell, no! Why do you call at such an hour?" As I put down the receiver, I heard, "Doc, I got a deadline to make." It wasn't easy for me to go back to sleep. I kept thinking: Why wouldn't I abort a woman who carried Sherri Finkbine's odds of producing a phocamelia (the word's Greek origin means seal), a child with arms and legs replaced by flipperlike extremities? I was sincerely convinced of the wisdom of aborting such cases. But I shunned the notoriety of a newspaper-sponsored abortion, and I was discouraged

Dr. Alan Guttmacher, surgeon, obstetrician, and gynecologist, is author of several books on birth control including Planning Your Family: The Complete Guide to Contraception and Fertility *(Macmillan). This article first appeared in* McCall's *magazine (April 1968), and is reprinted here through the courtesy of the author.*

by the forbidding logistics of getting a hospital bed
for Mrs. Finkbine. Most first-class New York hospitals
have established house rules to discourage abortion, so
they can boast of its low incidence—perhaps two, certainly no more than five, induced abortions per 1,000
live births. My own hospital would admit no patient
for abortion who had no previous medical association
with our staff. In these wakeful hours I had little ad-
miration for my own timidity or the timidity of my
medical colleagues. Mrs. Finkbine went to Stockholm's Karolinska Hospital and was humanely aborted
of a phocamelia fetus.

Several years ago, a distraught young woman
came to my office seeking abortion. She lived in a Brooklyn ground-floor apartment with its back yard opening
into the kitchen. Her story was that one day as she was
ironing, with her baby in the crib beside her and the
radio playing full blast, a hand was suddenly thrust
over her face, and she was wrestled to the floor and
forced to consent to rape, on threat of harm to her
child. She called her husband immediately, and he no-
tified the authorities. Several days later, a man she identified as the rapist was caught by a policeman husband
as the assailant was about to rape his wife.

When my patient found herself pregnant, she and
her husband went to the Brooklyn district attorney, re-
questing her admission to a municipal hospital for
abortion. He was sympathetic, but stated that he was
unable to help her because the law of the State of New
York permits abortion only to "preserve the life" of
the pregnant woman and her survival was not jeop-
ardized by continuation of pregnancy. The poor
woman rang the doorbells of several Brooklyn physicians, seeking legal abortion without success, so she
crossed the river to Manhattan. I verified the story with
the police, and despite my indignation, I was power-
less to abort her, since the large voluntary hospital in

which I worked did not permit abortion for rape. I telephoned several other professors of obstetrics and found one, ironically in Brooklyn, who did his private operating in a small hospital that permitted thera-peutic abortion in proved rape cases. He charged the unfortunate woman no fee for his services.

Within the past month, an obstetrician friend from Connecticut telephoned seeking help for his un-married, seventeen-year-old high-school daughter, who was pregnant. I referred him to an excellent Japanese physician, who had served an American residency with me. A million legal abortions are done each year in Japan, of which 1,000 are for Americans.

These three stories demonstrate the chaos, incon-sistency, and unsatisfactory state of current abortion practice in the United States. By comparison, other areas of medical practice are relatively neat, uniform, and free of legal surveillance and control.

Present abortion statutes make hypocrites of the medical profession. It is estimated that 70 percent of our million or so annual illegal abortions are done by physicians—some full-time operators, others part-time workers who want to pick up quick cash, for abor-tion fees must always be paid in cash. A full-time med-ical abortionist in a medium-size city showed me a little black book in which he listed the names of 300 refer-ring physicians. It read like a medical *Who's Who* of the area. The professional abortionists I have known vary in character and outlook, but all have two things in common. Their services are never free, and each thinks of himself as a knight in white armor rescuing ladies in distress. If they didn't, they could not live with themselves, for other doctors usually treat them as pariahs.

The fact that there are no free illegal abortions, no clinic type of setup, makes for the rankest discrim-ination. Abortion patients generally get what they pay for. A high-priced abortion is usually safely performed by a professional medical abortionist or a qualified part-time physician, frequently an obstetrician. A low fee is likely to employ some paramedical person, a hospital orderly or nurse, and is of doubtful safety. The lowest investment results in self-induction by means of a bougie, slippery-elm stick, hatpin, etc., or perhaps the cooperative effort of a kindly neighbor, who aids in the use of the same weapons. The danger in this category is great. The disproportionately high incidence of Negro abortion fatalities year after year in New York City reflects the correlation between pocketbook and safety in this sordid mess. Then, too, how does one find a medical abortionist? There are no easy or universal rules. Perhaps the lucky searcher has access to the telephone number of ''Mr. Frank'' in a middling-size town and has been instructed that the password is ''Evelyn referred me.''

Even the 10,000 legal abortions done in our hospitals are discriminatory. In a study I did in 1958, the therapeutic—or legal—abortion rate among hospitals in New York City was 2.5 per 1,000 live births among private patients and 0.5 among clinic patients. The pooled statistics of eleven large hospitals on the Eastern Seaboard showed a legal-abortion rate among their white patients of 2.9 per 1,000 live births and among non-whites of 0.08.

There are three possible solutions. First, law enforcement can be stepped up, and illegal abortion, the third largest U.S. racket after gambling and narcotics, can get its wings clipped. In regard to legal abortion, State Boards of Medical Examiners can see that each physician lives up to the exact letter of his state law; in 47 states abortion can still be performed only to save a woman's life. A second possibility is to repeal all abortion laws, permitting abortion on demand, the only control being imposed by the patient's conscience.

Third, existing restrictive laws could be modified and liberalized, as they were during 1967 in Colorado, North Carolina, and California.

What's wrong with the solution of rigid enforcement of existing statues? First, it is impossible. People at all levels oppose our abortion laws, and in a democracy when the majority opposes a law, it becomes unenforceable. According to the National Opinion Research Center, 71 percent of Americans favor legal abortion if a woman's health is endangered by pregnancy, 56 percent in rape cases, and 55 percent if there is a strong likelihood that the baby may be born with a serious defect. Among Catholics, 58 percent favor legal abortion if there is danger to life and 46 percent approve it for rape. Of the 40,089 U.S. physicians who answered a survey by *Modern Medicine* last spring, 87 percent favor liberalizing the laws—49 percent of Catholic, in contrast to 93 percent of non-Catholic, physicians. Readers who remember 1920 to 1933 recall the travesty made of the Volstead Prohibition Act because most people did not believe in it. Similarly, abortion statutes are out of step with our times. The body politic does not want their rigid enforcement; they want their liberalization.

Second, as a physician I strongly oppose literal interpretation and rigid enforcement of the existing abortion statutes. Through the loophole of individual interpretation by hospitals and physicians, a small proportion of the patients who in my eyes merit legal abortion somehow obtain it; but if we were to tighten the screws of the law, even they would be deprived of such beneficent help. With the rapid strides of modern medicine, few women today require abortion "to preserve life." In yesteryear it was common necessity. In the late 'twenties and early 'thirties I not infrequently aborted women with serious heart disease, extensive tuberculosis, poorly functioning kidneys, or intractable vomiting in early gestation, to prevent their death, but not today.

In 1963 I published a study of abortions done from 1953 through 1960 at the Mount Sinai Hospital in New York City and the University of Pennsylvania Hospital in Philadelphia. In the combined experience of both institutions, there was not a single abortion done for vomiting. Nine percent of 291 abortions were done for heart trouble, and slightly over two percent each for tuberculosis and kidney disease. In truth, the vast majority of the 291 abortions in these outstanding hospitals with impeccable reputations were actually not essential to "preserve" the woman's life and therefore were strictly illegal. Forty-one percent were done for emotional and psychiatric disturbances and 24 percent to spare a couple the likelihood of an abnormal child resulting from German measles in early pregnancy. If we cannot change the law, let's keep on doing as we are doing. Don't let us regress.

Third, there would be general opposition to the harassment or elimination of the illegal abortionist, particularly if he is safe. A good abortionist is viewed as a social necessity, as was the bootlegger during Prohibition who did not dispense hooch with wood alcohol. In brazen hypocrisy, our culture has declared most abortions illegal; but at the same time we try to protect those who resort to abortion, as well as their illegal perpetrators. Herman Schwartz, professor of law at the University of Buffalo, in a recent article has well summarized the current situation. "Our treatment of abortion is one more example of social hypocrisy— legal condemnation which appeases our Puritanism, and silent non-enforcement which accepts the realities. The result . . . hundreds of thousands of decent people forced into willful defiance of the law."

There are astonishingly few prosecutions compared to the vast number of abortions performed. According to the law, the patient herself is guilty of a felony, as are those associated with the "crime," such as a referring physician. However, as far as I know, neither is ever prosecuted. In the infrequent instances when abortionists are brought to trial, non-medical abortionists may get moderate sentences; but the courts are lenient with M.D.s, usually putting the offender on probation or giving him a light sentence. Perhaps they are lenient because the doctor is additionally penalized by his sanctimonious colleagues who sit on boards of medical examiners, some members of which no doubt have referred patients to him. These boards either permanently or temporarily revoke his license to practice. The leading medical abortionist in a community I knew well was given a light jail sentence, and within a few months a respected member of the same local medical fraternity was given a similar sentence for income-tax evasion. Both were released at about the same time. With, to me, a baffling sense of justice by the examiner, the abortionist was never allowed to practice again, while the tax dodger was permitted to go back to work immediately. I know an abortionist who was given a four-month sentence, and he divided his time between assistant jail physician, which permitted him to sleep in the jail's hospital, and driver of the milk truck, which gave him the chance to have daily lunch with his family.

The second possible solution is repeal of all abortion laws, transferring the matter of abortion from law to medicine. In the presence of highly permissive medical sanctions, this would mean abortion on demand. Let us see what is right and what is wrong in permitting a woman full choice in determining whether or not she will remain pregnant.

Since the woman has to bear and rear the child, who is more capable of choosing between birth and abortion? Childbirth is a personal experience and as such involves neither church nor state. At long last, women have become emancipated from the chaperonage of church and state in the prevention of pregnancy through use of contraceptives. Birth control is now viewed as a basic human right. Should she not enjoy equal freedom in the elimination of a pregnancy once begun? Philosophically there is very little moral difference between the prevention of pregnancy by contraception, abortion, or sterilization. Then, too, is not the perpetuation of the stricture on abortion in Christian lands an inheritance of the warped attitude toward sex stemming from Saint Augustine? In sum and substance: "Woman, you have enjoyed your carnal pleasure. Now do penance by paying for it." Perhaps the reason no similar penalty is exacted of the male, as Marya Mannes points out, is that abortion laws are the work of "the inseminators, not the bearers."

Abortion on demand would greatly speed the goal of making each child a wanted child, which would reduce the vast army of neglected and rejected children and cut by half the 300,000 illegitimate children born in this country each year. Then, too, it would take the powder out of shotgun marriages, which contribute so heavily to the inordinately high divorce rate among teen-age brides.

Abortion on demand would almost eliminate the racket of illegal abortion and thereby in large part get rid of one of the many flagrant practices that foment disrespect for law. It would also reduce social, economic, and ethnic discrimination in an important segment of medical care and protect the life and health of hundreds of thousands of women each year by substituting a safe medical procedure for an unsafe one.

This is not theory; this is fact. In a four-year period, 1961–1964, one million legal abortions under the supervision of the state were reported officially from Hungary and Czechoslovakia with 25 deaths, a rate of 2.5 per 100,000. In these countries, legal abortion imposes one twentieth of the maternal hazard of childbirth. Deaths from illegal abortion have declined over 80 percent in Hungary since the institution of abortion on demand. The reason that illegal abortions and deaths from illegal abortions have not been totally eliminated is that the government does not permit abortion after the twelfth week unless there is true medical necessity, and some Hungarian women insist on abortion for reasons other than health after the third month. Also, abortions are done openly in East Europe in government hospitals, and some women in Communist countries are reluctant to publicize their abortions. If ever there is abortion on demand in the United States, it will be up to the medical profession in each state to determine whether we shall continue the present private-patient versus clinic-patient differential, the former with its relative secrecy, the latter with its unconcealed openness.

The introduction of abortion on demand would even lower further the U.S. birth rate from 18 per 1,000, its current level. World over, an immediate decline in birth rate has been one of the most striking and consistent results of easily obtained legal abortion. When Japan introduced its permissive abortion law in 1948, it had a birth rate of 34.5 per 1,000; within two years the rate declined dramatically to 20, and over the past several years has been stationary around 18. Hungary had a birth rate of 23 in the mid-fifties, when it introduced abortion on demand, and since 1962 it has consistently had a rate of 13, the world's lowest. Romania instituted abortion on demand in 1957, when its birth rate was 22, and by 1965 it had declined to 14.5, the second lowest in the world. In 1966, to stimulate births, Romania repealed its 1957 law and substituted a law that restricts abortion to women over 45 years of age, to mothers supporting four or more living children, and to medical, eugenic, and humanitarian indications, the last a commonly employed euphemism for rape and incest. I am curious to know whether the new law will stimulate births or illegal abortions. Time will soon tell.

Annual U.S. population growth has slowed from a rate of 1.7 percent in 1957 to one percent. In terms of air pollution, water contamination, urban congestion, increasing unemployment, and other indices, even this rate of growth is still too rapid. If the introduction of abortion on demand would significantly reduce the U.S. population dynamics, many would applaud the result.

What are the arguments against abortion on demand?

Some claim that abortion is murder and therefore should never be performed or, if done, only in those rare cases in which continuation of pregnancy may cost a woman her life. Those who claim abortion is murder believe it immoral and decadent to sanction legal termination of early pregnancy because a woman elects not to bear a child.

The lines have been drawn between the theists and the humanists—one defending every fetus' inviolable right to be born, the other holding that those already born must be granted precedence and allowed to protect themselves against an unwanted pregnancy. The fact that 71 percent of Americans—*including 87 percent of U.S. physicians*—favor extension of the practice of legal abortion attests that the humanists are winning over the deists; but the fact that only three states have broadened their abortion laws shows that the deists are giving ground slowly and begrudgingly.

I am strongly of the opinion that abortion is not murder. From my viewpoint, destruction of the early conceptus differs in no essential from destruction of the sperm cell or egg cell before the act of fertilization.

No one mourns for a sperm killed by a spermatoxic contraceptive cream or an ovum permitted to die twelve hours after ovulation, because the woman from whose ovary it came knew how to prevent its survival by practicing the rhythm technique. Sperm and egg are living cells before fertilization; otherwise, conception could not occur. In the continuum of living matter they remain living cells with and after fertilization.

I cannot allow myself the impious thought that the godhead rides each spermatozoan like a horseman and enters the egg cell bestowing upon it the sanctification of the godhead. To me, an early conception is not a human being created in God's image; it is a potential human being in man's image. It is a mass of undifferentiated cells, which sort themselves into a specific pattern according to the blueprint architected by the RNA given them through inheritance from each parent. The difference between an early embryo and a living person is immense. The embryo has no consciousness, no life experience, no previous association with fellow humans. Therefore, equating the elimination of a mass of developing cells with infanticide, euthanasia, and genocide is offensive and patently fallacious. The charge that liberalization of abortion laws will inevitably lead to these practices is illogical and wickedly inflammatory. Has liberalization of divorce laws led to the abolition of marriage?

For me the end point when abortion is no longer permissible is not governed by intangibles like the exact day or week when the fetus is assumed to receive its soul or when its mind is thought first to function, but by pure medical considerations. Rarely a twenty-six-week fetus lives after a natural birth, and a surviving fetus so small, fragile, and immature has grave likelihood of serious brain damage. Therefore to forestall this possibility I feel a full four-week leeway should be given in producing an aborted fetus. Therefore, I approve of abortion up to the twenty-second week, but not beyond. From the technical viewpoint of the operator, abortion before the twelfth week of pregnancy is simple and virtually danger-free, and between weeks twelve and twenty-two more complicated and not without hazard.

Like all arguments charged with such deep emotional content, especially arguments of a philosophical-moral nature incapable of proof by experiment, it is almost impossible to convert minds already committed. Thoughtful men of good will who believe that abortion is murder almost certainly will not be persuaded by the preceding paragraphs that it is not murder. I fully respect their opinion, but quickly confess that arguments by theists will fail to change my stand. It is largely to uncommitted minds that my discussion is addressed.

A second argument against abortion on demand is that it is likely to change many basic human values. Perhaps it does, but I see no evidence of it. Visits to Japan and Yugoslavia have revealed no essential differences between human values and moral judgments there and in America. There seems to be the same sense of family unity with the same worshipful parental attachment to young children. Births, marriages, deaths have the same importance.

A third objection to unlimited abortion is the report of frequent undesirable psychic and physical reactions following its legal performance. I bring this matter up to lay a ghost. Three excellent studies, published during 1966, by Niswander and Patterson, Peck and Marcus, and Baird all show that "in women who had a pregnancy terminated, psychiatric and neurotic symptoms were no more common than one might expect in the population generally." In his study, Sir Dougald Baird, who is a distinguished emeritus professor of obstetrics in Scotland, states: "In most unmarried women the crisis is resolved by termination of pregnancy, and the benefit is immediate and very pronounced. . . . In many young married women the effects of termination are equally gratifying . . . and the benefits to the whole marriage situation may be very considerable. In older married women who do not want more children and are strained to the breaking point by the occurrence of another pregnancy, the results of termination plus tubal ligation are most satisfactory. There is striking improvement in the woman's physical and mental health and in the well-being of the whole family.''

Despite the fact that I do not believe abortion is murder, that an unlimited frequency of legal abortion virtually eliminates the abortion racket, that I feel the woman should be the judge as to whether an early pregnancy should continue or be terminated, that easy abortion neither creates moral or sexual decadence nor is commonly associated with or followed by undesirable physical, psychic, or emotional complications, I oppose abortion on demand, at least now for the United States. There are several reasons.

First, the public does not want it. According to the poll of the National Opinion Research Center, only 20 percent of Americans favor abortion for single women and only 17 percent for mothers who do not want more children—the main seekers of abortion. In a democracy, it is safer to evolve radical social change by evolution than by revolution. If we succeed in greatly liberalizing all fifty state statutes by 1975, then perhaps in the last decade of the century state after state will be prepared to remove abortion from all legal controls. To be sure, by 1990 this may no longer be necessary, for if before then a safe, effective pill is discovered that any woman can take on the twenty-fifth day of a menstrual cycle and it will bring on her period three days later, whether or not she is pregnant, the matter of repealing abortion laws becomes strictly an academic matter. Such a pill has not been perfected, but work along this line is being carried on at the Karolinska Institute in Stockholm and probably elsewhere. Eventual success is likely.

From the political viewpoint, state legislators do not lead their electorate in matters involving social change; they follow. Therefore, if people feel, as I do, that current abortion statutes are hideously punitive, discriminatory, archaic, and nonworkable, they will put their shoulders to the wheel of change rather than attempt the impossible task of overturning the vehicle before it becomes unmired.

Second, I oppose abortion on demand because it reduces the necessity to use effective contraception, and as a physician I feel it is better physically and psychically to prevent pregnancy than to terminate it through abortion. For example, since abortion is normally not carried out until a woman is about two months pregnant, it does not eliminate the queasiness so frequently felt in early pregnancy. In countries like Japan, contraception has a difficult task in gaining acceptance. I learned from Japanese colleagues that it is not uncommon for women to have two abortions a year, and three a year are far from unknown.

Third, abortion on demand relieves the male of all responsibility in the sphere of pregnancy control. He becomes a coital animal without necessity to think of consequences—not far removed from the status of a bull. To be sure, the birth-control pill has almost relegated him to the same brute position, but at least he still has the responsibility to ask his wife, "Did you take your pill today?"

Since I oppose current restrictive abortion laws as well as their repeal, I favor liberation of existing laws. The movement toward liberalization received great impetus when the American Law Institute (ALI), a committee of eminent judges, lawyers, and legal teachers and scholars, framed a new abortion statute in 1959 as part of a revised penal code, which was adopted by them officially in 1962. Professor Herbert Wechsler, of the Columbia Law School, was the chief architect of the part of the code that dealt with abortion. The ALI code states that termination of pregnancy may be performed only in a licensed hospital after certification in writing by two physicians, one of whom may be the operator, that the circumstances they believe to justify the abortion are on one of three grounds: (1) there is substantial risk that the continuation of pregnancy would gravely impair the physical or mental health of the mother; (2) the child would be born with grave physical or mental defect; (3) the pregnancy resulted from rape, incest, or other felonious intercourse (intercourse, with or without consent, with a child under 16).

During 1967, abortion-reform bills were presented before 28 state legislatures, all of them either the exact copy of the ALI code or with minor modifications. Colorado in April, 1967, was the first state to enact a liberalized abortion bill. It differs from the ALI code only in that it requires a hospital committee of three physicians to give unanimous approval, instead of any two physicians. North Carolina, the next state to amend its abortion law, added a four-month residency clause to the ALI code, to prevent patients from flocking to North Carolina for abortion. California passed a bill including maternal health and sex crime, but excluding fetal indications, since Governor Reagan stated that he would absolutely veto any bill including them. Mississippi simply added rape to its existing preservation-of-life law—hardly significant liberalization. It is anticipated that many states will reintroduce the ALI code or a modification of it in 1968. Hopefully, several, including New York's bill, will be reported out of committee to the floor of the legislature, and some will pass, if not this year, next year or the year after that.

Great Britain, after months of debate, "in a triumph for humanity and common sense," according to Professor Alan Parkes, Cambridge zoologist, passed and signed into law on October 27, 1967, a far more liberal bill than any enacted by a U.S. state. The bill will become operational April 27. Then abortion will be legal if two doctors agree that continuance of pregnancy would involve risk to the life of the pregnant woman or injury to her physical or mental health or to any existing children. In making such a determination, "the pregnant woman's actual or reasonably foreseeable environment" may be taken into account. The bill also includes a section permitting abortion if there is "substantial risk that if the child were born it would suffer from physical or mental abnormalities" sufficiently severe to cause it "to be seriously handicapped."

The distinctive feature of the bill is naming, as a ground for abortion, "risk to the physical or mental health of any existing children," including the effect an additional child would have on the environment of children already born. This allows consideration of overcrowding, inadequate housing, strain on the mother, and similar factors.

In my opinion, the code of the American Law Institute is too restrictive, not so much from the medical as from the social point of view. I would include all that it now includes—substantial risk to maternal physical or mental health, eugenic indications, and impregnation resulting from sex crime—and would add the following:

(1) Unmarried females of 18 or under.

(2) Mothers already caring for three or more children.

(3) Women of forty or more.

(4) Drug addicts or severe alcoholics.

(5) Women with subnormal mentality incapable of providing satisfactory parental care.

(6) Emotionally disturbed parents unable to cope with another child.

These recommendations may seem unnecessarily specific, especially in view of the vague verbiage of the new English law; but having practiced obstetrics and gynecology for over three decades, I realize that U.S. physicians seek exact guidelines for whom they may or may not legally abort. Otherwise, their timidity and that of the hospitals in which they practice will incubate splendid inaction.

A PUBLIC HEALTH OFFICIAL LOOKS AT ABORTION

BY DR. HERBERT RATNER

Back in 1860, Dr. Oliver Wendell Holmes delivered an address before the Massachusetts Medical Society entitled *Currents and Counter-Currents in Medical Science.* This address was an endeavor to set up a counter-current to reverse the excessive therapeutic activity characteristic of the physician. Dr. Holmes attributed this excess, in great part, to the immense outside pressure from the public which was forcing the physician to active intervention of some kind; and, in smaller part, to the physician's tendency to self-delusion concerning his accomplishments. In the course of developing his thesis, Dr. Holmes gave us one of those profound, timeless insights that deserve our most sober consideration as we attempt to render a professional judgment concerning the wisdom of extending indications for induced abortions.

Herbert Ratner, M.D., Director of the Public Health Department, Oak Park, Illinois, is widely known for his Interview on Medicine *published in 1962 by the Center for the Study of Democratic Institutions as one of a series of* Interviews on the American Character.

"A Public Health Official Looks at Abortion" originally appeared in the Winter 1968 issue of Child and Family *and is reprinted here through the courtesy of the publisher.*

He called attention to the unsuspected, close "relation between the medical sciences and the conditions of society and the general thought of our time" with this statement: that although "theoretically medicine ought to go on its own straightforward inductive path without regard to changes of government or to fluctuations of public opinion . . . the truth is that medicine, professionally founded on observation, is as sensitive to outside influences, political, religious, philosophical, imaginative, as is the barometer to the changes of atmospheric density."

Dr. Holmes describes this susceptibility of medicine to nonmedical factors and urges the physician who has any respect for his profession to firmly adhere to the medical principles of his science and art.

A similar thought expressed more recently by two leading social scientists in a book entitled *Human Behavior: An Inventory of Scientific Findings* provides a contemporary counterpart which also deserves our sober consideration.

This is *Time's* version of the book's conclusion:

Today's behavioral man is "a depressing creature with a vast talent for distorting reality because of psychological needs. (He) thinks what fits his wishes, says what pleases his peers, avoids conflict and protects his neuroses. He votes with his friends, wants what he has to work for, and thinks his group or organization ranks higher than it does. If threatened with disillusionment, he simply slides into fantasy, and reality pays the price."

Fictitious statistics

The following are some illustrations of this tendency in scientists (and the mass communicators who follow them) "to distort reality to fit their wishes."

1. The misstatement that there are ten thousand deaths a year from illegal abortion.

But the fact, as established at a three day Planned Parenthood Conference of 43 experts and as reported by Dr. Mary Calderone, its medical director at the time, is:

"I can tell you that in 1957 there were only 260 deaths in the whole country attributed to abortion of any kind. Abortion is no longer a dangerous procedure, and this applies not just to therapeutic abortions as done in hospitals, but also to so-called illegal abortions. . . ."

That was the figure for 1957. In 1963, for the U.S. as a whole, there were 275 deaths attributed to abortion of any kind. Of these deaths only 114 were due to abortions that were criminal, self-induced, or without legal indications. Total maternal deaths for the U.S. in 1963—and this includes all other maternal deaths as well as abortion deaths—only numbered 1400.

What makes the statistic of 10,000 deaths yearly somewhat outlandish is that the total number of deaths of women in the reproductive age period is only, mind you, only 50,000 yearly. If the 10,000 figure were correct, it would mean that one out of five women between the ages of 15 and 45 who die dies of an abortion. This hardly leaves room for deaths from other causes. Deaths from cancer, cardiovascular and kidney disease number by themselves about half of the 50,000 deaths of women between the ages of 15 and 45. Deaths from automobile and other accidents number another 7,000. Additionally there are lesser numbers of deaths from influenza and pneumonia, cirrhosis of the liver, diabetes, tuberculosis and all of the numerous other causes. It is a preposterous figure and should not be used, least of all by the medical profession which has a responsibility to speak accurately. The figure, incidentally, is extrapolated from some highly unrepresentative data collected from patients attending a New York City birth control clinic in the pre-antibiotic years of 1925–1929.

2. The misstatement that there are a million or a million and a half illegal abortions a year.

But this is what a special committee on abortion, chaired by Dr. Christopher Tietze and including Dr. Alan Guttmacher, says: "A plausible estimate of the frequency of induced abortion in the U.S. could be as low as 200,000 and as high as 1,200,000, depending upon the assumptions made . . . and the assessment of bias. *There is no objective basis for the selection of a particular figure between these two estimates as an approximation of the actual frequency.*" (italics added)

Since there were only 3,500,000 live births in the U.S. in 1966, and since contraception has long been available to 5/6ths of all women at reproductive age, the figure of one million abortions yearly, which gives a ratio of abortions to live births of 1 to 3.5, seems highly improbable. In Sweden where abortion is legalized and where abortion has become a cultural pattern, the rate of abortion to live births in 1963 was only 1 to 31, or ninefold less.

Fanciful embryology

The same distortion of reality occurs when we move from statistics to the science of embryology. Abortion protagonists refer to the unborn offspring as a part of the mother not significantly different from sperm or egg, a piece of tissue, an inchoate being, a small mass of cells, a blob, a parasite, a tumor.

When *Life* editorializes in favor of abortion, it states, "A fetus is a living body—but not a human being until birth." However, in their earlier unique pictorial story, *The Drama of Life Before Birth, Life* states, "The birth of a human *really* occurs at the moment the mother's egg cell is fertilized by one of the father's sperm cells." (italics added)

We find a similar situation with the *New York Times*. A recent article, *The New Medical Specialty, Fetology—The World of the Unborn*, states, "Scientists generally agree (that at) the coming together of egg and sperm . . . conception takes place (and) a new life . . . a new human being . . . begins." It refers to it as a "small miracle." This scientific fact, however, is not reflected in its editorial pages.

Another example of the scientist's capacity to distort reality is Dr. Alan Guttmacher's recent testimony before the New York State Assembly Committees on Code and Health that legal abortions are "magnificently safe." (When we can no longer say this about an aspirin tablet, one wonders what miracle of science permits us to say it about an abortion.) Contrarily, however, Dr. Christopher Tietze, director of research for the National Committee on Maternal Health, and a close working colleague of Dr. Guttmacher, is reported as saying something quite different at Johns Hopkins University. He urged that "an international research effort be undertaken to find safe and simple methods of terminating pregnancy."

Finally, I would like to call attention to a particularly grievous error which appeared in the *Chicago Daily News* in its recent series on abortion. It inferred that Hippocrates was a hypocrite; that at the high level of pious declaration he said one thing, but in the daily expediencies of practice he did another. The *News* contrasted a case history (in which Hippocrates helped a young lady to abort) to his great oath (in which he clearly and unequivocally speaks against abortion). But there is no such case history written by Hippocrates, and the medical profession has a right to resent the slandering of this great pagan physician who gave medicine its moral imprint and eternal dedication to the preservation of life and who first distinguished medicine as a profession from that of a technology or trade. The error originated with Dr. Frederick Taussig in his book, *The Medical and Social Aspects of Abortion*, published in 1936, and has been repeated with great avidity and regularity by proponents of abortion who fail to distinguish fiction from fact.

These are just a few examples of how we get carried away today by our desires and enthusiasms. The problem continues as we make claims for future benefits to be derived from a relaxation of the abortion laws. Last fall, at the annual meeting of the American Public Health Association in San Francisco, Dr. Christopher Tietze admonished us, before embarking on any changes of abortion laws, to study the experiences of other countries, from which we have much to learn.

These are some of the utilitarian and pragmatic things we can learn.

Case histories from abroad

1. That where abortion laws are relaxed, contraception is discarded or ignored. This seems to be a universal phenomenon. Actually, abortion now is the most widely used single method of birth control throughout the world, according to Prof. Ronald Freedman. Rather than take a powerful, disruptive, dangerous hormone pill, or carry a permanent foreign body inside, or use diaphragms or jellies, women prefer to accept nature as it is. In Japan women who are active sexually and don't want babies find it simpler to have abortions approximately every eight months until sterility sets in.

Dr. Franc Novak of Yugoslavia devoted an entire talk to this subject at the Singapore Conference of

International Planned Parenthood. Under the title, *"Why Does Contraception Meet So Many Difficulties in Superseding Abortions?"* Dr. Novak said the following:

"In spite of great needs, contraception is very slow in spreading while abortions are on a steady increase, threatening to become a real epidemic. Why do women not prefer contraception, which is simpler and less unpleasant, to abortion? In our country, there are no visible obstacles to modern contraception; on the contrary, it is even supported, encouraged and stimulated. In a socialist society prophylaxis stands in the foreground of medical thinking and acting. It is included in our health service whose duty is to put it into practice. . . . Our propaganda meets with no obstacles. Lectures, pamphlets, films, radio and television are at our disposal—and yet our progress is slow. Religion represents no obstacles in our country. . . . It seems that the greatest obstacle to the spread of contraception lies in liberal permission of artificial abortions. Through widespread abortions a state of mind is created with women that abortion represents the chief means for planned parenthood."

At the same meeting Dr. Hans Harmsen of Western Germany stated that legalization of abortion increased the pregnancy rate, and Dr. Tietze added that with abortion legislation, contraceptives were practiced in a more slipshod manner.

The conclusion is clear. Relaxation of the abortion laws will stimulate the need for more abortions and will increase rather than decrease the abortion problem.

2. Contrary to general belief and propaganda, liberalized indications for abortion along the lines envisaged for the United States in imitation of Sweden will *not* reduce the incidence of criminal abortions as alleged. Dr. Tietze in his San Francisco paper entitled, *Abortion In Europe*, states that although "one of the

major goals of the liberalization of abortion laws in
Scandinavia was to reduce the incidence of illegal abortion,'' this was not accomplished. Rather, as we know
from a variety of sources, both criminal and total abortions increased.

Even were we to permit abortion on demand as
in the Eastern European countries, which would result
in ''spectacular increases in the incidence of legal abortions'' as compared to Sweden, even then criminal abortion would still persist.

Let me illustrate this with Hungary, which has
the highest rate of legal abortions and where abortion
is available on request. Whereas for each 1000 live
births in Sweden there are only 32 legal abortions, in
Hungary for each 1000 live births there are 1400
legal abortions, more abortions than births, and 44
times the Swedish number. For the U.S. this would be
close to five million legal abortions annually as against
three and half million live births. Despite this massive
blood bath, which Dr. Hartman tells me is resulting in
increased depressive reactions and breakdowns among
guilt-ridden Hungarian physicians, illegal abortion remains. Dr. Tietze thinks illegal abortion survives because of the ''relative lack of privacy of the official procedure.'' It seems apparent then that anyone knowing
these figures would be less than honest, and to some
extent cruel, if he continued to urge a change in abortion laws along the lines of the so-called model code of
the American Law Institute, for the purpose of rescuing women from criminal abortions.

3. To be most pragmatic, let us not forget that
the liberty to abort makes the physician more like a
god than is good for him. Abortions are also lucrative.
We've experienced the prevalence of unnecessary operations and the invasiveness of the attitude that jus-
tifies them. We know that in the effort to please patients some of the profession have a great talent for

descending to the lowest common denominator. If today some licensed physicians practicing in approved hospitals disregard both the letter and the spirit of the legal therapeutic abortion by performing abortions that are in no way "necessary for the preservation of the woman's life," what reason is there to think that tomorrow were the law made more permissive and the indications more tenuous, physicians would be more respectful of the law? We will again hear the old refrain by an even larger chorus, "If I don't do it somebody else will." But this time we will be dealing with delicate decisions of life and death.

4. Increased numbers of abortions universally result in increased impairment of both physical and mental health. That is why none of the countries where abortions have been extended are happy about their high and increasing abortion rates.

Dr. Novak from Yugoslavia in the article referred to above simply refers to "The evil consequences of liberally permitted abortions. . . ." Dr. Klinger of the Hungarian Central Office of Statistics commenting on the Eastern European experience states, ". . . induced abortion is . . . one of the chief means of birth control. Its deleterious effect on health is sufficient reason to change the present-day situation.

"The great Soviet experiment of free abortion, which continued for eight years after the revolution, still affords us the best evidence of physical injury following the operation," according to Dr. Muller. Dr. DeLee reports the morbidity of that experience as follows: "Russia, which has legalized abortion has completely reversed its position under the accumulated bad experience with 140,000 such operations a year. The authorities call the practice a serious psychic, moral and social evil and inherently dangerous even when performed *lege artis*. They found trauma—uterine perforation, cervical laceration and stenosis, parametritis,

etc.—ectopic pregnancy and biological trauma—amen-
orrhea, sterility, endocrinopathies. Subsequent labor
was more often pathologic: placenta praevia, atonia
uteri, adherent placenta, postpartum hemorrhage and
postpartum fever (32%)."

At the Singapore meeting of International
Planned Parenthood, Dr. Nobuo Shinozaki, of the Japanese Ministry of Health and Welfare, made these re-
vealing remarks about abortion and the quality of living in Japan.

"To be honest, in spite of the increasing economic
development, our national life is not by comparison so
much happier. . . . Certainly the technical advance since
the war has been remarkable, but it does not follow
that parallel improvements have been made in the
actual people. . . . In short, modern civilization or culture has caused human beings to modify human nature to part of a machine, which is toward an 'alienation' of the human being. As a result, we find in
Japan that death by accident or suicide is highest in
the under 24 year age group. To be added to this is
the damage to the nervous system and sexual problems,
especially sexual apathy and impotence. The practice
of family planning is inevitable and it has a very important role in every era, but where it combines with
other factors to ignore the quality of human life it must
be reassessed. In conclusion I recall the saying, 'The
longest way round is often the shortest way home.' "

The responsible physician

I will close with some observations as a public
health officer who shares with other physicians the obligation of his profession to serve all human beings not
only equally, but equally *well*. I add *well* to *equally*,
because it has long been known that private patients

are the recipients of more meddlesome midwifery than ward patients—to use the famous phrase of a famous Chicago obstetrician, Dr. Rudolph Holmes. If affluent patients have a greater incidence of induced labors or induced abortions, it does not follow that true democracy demands that the poor also reap this overabundance. In medicine, we want human beings to share the beneficial, not the detrimental. And when we talk about human beings we mean all human beings; not simply the rich and not simply the adult.

It took a long time to get the child into the obstetrical picture. In the early fifties we enlarged the concept of the American Association for Maternal Welfare to include Child Welfare. Today the good obstetrician no longer doubts that in pregnancy he serves two patients. If he has doubts, the good pediatrician will remind him. And if we do have a defective fetus, it is not his annihilation but his care, cure and rehabilitation which is the mark of the good physician and the road to medical progress.

Let us not be misled by the Latin term *fetus*. When translated into English all it means is *the young one, the young in the womb, the unborn offspring*. If we attend to the etymology of *infant*, which means *not to speak*, we can see that the fetus is even more of an infant than the infant; for it can't even cry, or if it could it couldn't be heard. Who is there to speak in defense of this unborn infant but the physician?

If we have joined legislative forces *against* parents to combat the evil of the battered child syndrome, can we support a movement which makes permissive a medical partnership *with* parents which does the opposite—which extends to an earlier age what we forbid at a later age? Can we not see that what is advocated as therapeutic for the mother is hardly therapeutic for the child? After taking up the cudgel against the battered child syndrome are we now going to pick up the

curette and replace the extrauterine with the intra-
uterine battered child syndrome?

Mrs. Sherri Finkbine, of thalidomide fame, fran-
tically raced to get her abortion for she knew that once
she felt life, that once quickening took place, she would
never be able to go through with it. Aristotle also held
the position that abortion before quickening, but not
after, was permissible because of the absence of anima-
tion and therefore the animated soul. But surely the
modern doctor has traveled a long distance from the
third century B.C. and the embryology of Aristotle, and
beyond the lay person's understanding of when life is
present. The word doctor means teacher and a grave
teaching job confronts us.

For this we first of all need honesty—the honesty
of Planned Parenthood's pamphlet entitled, *Plan Your
Children for Health and Happiness*, which in answer to
the question, "Is birth control an abortion?" answers,
"Definitely not. An abortion kills the life of a baby
after it has begun. It is dangerous to your life and
health. It may make you sterile so that when you want
a child you cannot have it."

And we need the honesty of Dr. Mary Calderone
when she said in 1959, "Believe me, I am not for it
(indiscriminate abortion) for, aside from the fact that
abortion is the taking of a life, I am mindful of what
was brought out by our psychiatrists, that in almost
every case abortion, whether legal or illegal, is a traumatic experience that may have severe kickbacks later
on."

And secondly, we must profoundly grasp the im-
port of the proposed provision permitting the abortion
of an unborn offspring by virtue of a defect. This
represents a radical departure from the entire tradition
of medicine. It permits a physician to decide, on the
basis of his estimate of a defect, who is to live and
who is to die. It initiates the beginning of a brand new

end of medicine. To the perfective, preventive and curative ends we can now add Exterminative Medicine. When it will stop no one knows. The lessons of the Nazi era and the Nuremberg trials have obviously not been learned.

Perhaps Dr. Joseph DeLee, the former and great University of Chicago Lying-In medical director, the obstetrician whose pioneering work as guardian of maternal life and health catapulted Chicago obstetrics into world leadership, says it best.

He said it in a long editorial note in 1940. His remark is best appreciated in the light of an earlier editorial note that appeared in 1927.

In 1927 he stated bluntly, "The only thing I have to say about therapeutic abortions is that there are not enough done."

But appreciation of life becomes sweet with experience and age.

I close with his statement of 1940:

"All doctors (except abortionists) feel that the principles of the sanctity of human life, held since the time of the ancient Jews and Hippocrates and stubbornly defended by the Catholic Church are correct. And we are pained when placed before the necessity of sacrificing it. At the present time, when rivers of blood and tears of innocent men, women and children are flowing in most parts of the world, it seems silly to be contending over the right to live of an unknowable atom of human flesh in the uterus of a woman. No, it is not silly. On the contrary, it is of transcendent importance that there be in this chaotic world one high spot, however small, which is against the deluge of immorality that is sweeping over us. That we the medical profession hold to the principle of the sacredness of human life and of the right of the individual even though unborn is proof that humanity is not yet lost and that we may ultimately obtain salvation."

PRIVATE MORALITY

TABOOS
IN TWILIGHT

BY PAUL D. ZIMMERMAN

The old taboos are dead or dying. A new, more permissive society is taking shape. Its outlines are etched most prominently in the arts—in the increasing nudity and frankness of today's films, in the blunt, often obscene language seemingly endemic in American novels and plays, in the candid lyrics of pop songs and the undress of the avant-garde ballet, in erotic art and television talk shows, in freer fashions and franker advertising. And, behind this expanding permissiveness in the arts stands a society in transition, a society that has lost its consensus on such crucial issues as premarital sex and clerical celibacy, marriage, birth control and sex education; a society that cannot agree on standards of conduct, language and manners, on what can be seen and heard.

While artists and writers hail this new candor as a release from an era of Victorian repression and hypocrisy, many Americans are bewildered and con-

Paul D. Zimmerman, author of "Taboos in Twilight," is Associate Editor of Newsweek *magazine.*

This article first appeared in Newsweek *(Nov. 13, 1967)* © *Newsweek, Inc. November 1967 and is reprinted here with permission.*

cerned about the swiftness with which all the old restraints are losing their force. Mores are changing so
fast, in fact, that the biting, bitchy language of "Who's
Afraid of Virginia Woolf?," which caused Hollywood
to rewrite its Production Code only eighteen months
ago [1966], today sounds surprisingly tame. " 'Virginia
Woolf' is vanilla compared to the film version of
'Ulysses'," says Jack Valenti, president of the Motion
Picture Association of America, who has helped to
modernize a Hollywood Production Code that is already obsolete. "Films can't live in a vacuum. They
relate to the temper of the times, the postures of today."

These new postures alarm many citizens, psychologists and social thinkers who see in this rapid
destruction of taboos a dangerous swing toward irresponsible hedonism and, ultimately, social decay. "It
is the inevitable mark of decadence in our society,"
says British social commentator Malcolm Muggeridge.
"As our vitality ebbs, people reach out for vicarious
excitement, like the current sex mania in pop songs
and the popular press. At the decline and fall of the
Roman Empire, the works of Sappho, Catullus and Ovid
were celebrated. There is an analogy in that for us."

There are others, however, who reject the notion
that the new permissiveness is a sign of moral collapse.
"We are just beginning to discover what morality is all
about," says theater critic Kenneth Tynan. "It is concerned with how we behave toward each other, not
how much of our bodies we happen to display. There
will be no return to the horse and buggy or to full-
length skirts."

Change: Indeed, the revolution in manners and
morals that has produced a climate of candor is very
real and unlikely to reverse itself. "We're going to have
to live with a degree of freedom much greater than
anything we've known in the past," says Father Walter
J. Ong, the brilliant Jesuit theologian and author of

"The Presence of the Word." "Man can't just say anything goes and hope to get by. We're going to have to employ our minds and morals in determining that some things go and other things don't. We're going to have to constantly reassess the situation because the situation will always be changing."

It has changed more dramatically in the past year than in the preceding 50. The teen-age narrator of Norman Mailer's "Why Are We in Vietnam?" peppers the reader with a stream of profanity unparalleled in American letters. On stage in "The Beard," Billy the Kid and Jean Harlow assault each other with salvos of four-letter words, then end their sexual duel in an explicit act of oral intercourse. In "Scuba Duba," playwright Bruce Jay Friedman unleashes a bare-breasted floozie before sellout crowds. In "America Hurrah," giant dolls copulate onstage. And at Joseph Papp's exciting new theater, teen-agers in a musical called "Hair" sing gutter profanity with the cherubic straightforwardness of choir boys.

Across the U.S., audiences pack art houses and neighborhood theaters to watch the multiple orgasms of a seldom-clothed young Swedish actress in "I, a Woman." Italian director Antonioni breaks the taboo against head-on, total nudity in "Blow-Up," and Hollywood, in important films like "In the Heat of the Night" and "Bonnie and Clyde," shows its starlets bare to the waist.

Glossily mounted films such as "The Born Losers" and "The Penthouse" use excellent acting and shock techniques to reflect the violence and sex fever of the front pages. Gentle, white-haired old Spencer Tracy, in his last movie, "Guess Who's Coming to Dinner?" dismisses bigots with a terse "screw all those people." Alec Guinness, in "The Comedians," asks Richard Burton about Elizabeth Taylor: "You mean she's a good lay?" "Portrait of Jason," a remarkable voyage into the

twisted soul of a black male prostitute, compresses into
less than two hours all the raw language and candid
corners of life that today find free expression in almost
every independent U.S. film. And, in "Barbarella," a
film built around the endless seductions of a French
comic-strip heroine, Jane Fonda hops from one nude
scene to the next in celebration of the erotic life.

Best-selling literature, once reluctantly discreet, is
open and explicit about everything in the sexual spec-
trum from incest to inversion. "Valley of the Dolls,"
"The Adventurers" and "The Exhibitionist" use language once reserved to green-jacketed books smuggled
in from Paris. And these books—the works of Henry
Miller and the Marquis de Sade, "My Secret Life,"
"The Traveller's Companion Series" and "Story of O"
—today bring what used to be called hard-core pornography to the paperback rack at the corner drug store.
Even the intellectual press in Britain and the U.S., including mass-circulation magazines like *Playboy* and
Esquire, has been forced, in reporting the events of the
day, to use language once only read on privy walls.

Off: In pop music, the Rolling Stones sing "Let's
Spend the Night Together" while fans wear buttons
reading "Let's Lock Loins." TV viewers have seen
David Susskind talking frankly with homosexuals, as
well as wine and shaving-cream commercials chanting:
"Had any lately?" or "Take it off, take it all off."
Dance companies from Africa and San Francisco perform naked in New York. Erotic-art shows draw enormous crowds. Skirts escalate past knees and thighs.
Make-up is designed specifically to stay on in bed.
"We're living in a Babylonian society perhaps more
Babylonian than Babylon itself," says historian and
columnist Max Lerner. "It's what's called a late sen-
sate period. The emphasis in our society today is on the
senses and the release of the sensual. All the old codes
have been broken down."

This new freedom of expression is unlikely to reverse itself because the forces that have produced it are a permanent and irresistible part of modern life. The history of the arts itself has been a constant assault on forms and conventions to get at the essence of man and explore the deepest regions of his mind, spirit—and body. When James Joyce unlocked Molly Bloom's earthy, human, profane subconscious, he opened a Pandora's box that has become the common property of today's novelists and filmmakers, artists, potboilers and pornographers.

"What was once the realm of private knowledge has become public knowledge," says Father John M. Culkin, director of communications at Fordham and a disciple of media-master Marshall McLuhan. "Perhaps there's too much honesty but there's no doubt that these things have become part of the public domain." And this articulation of the inner self and man's own sexuality is not limited to artists alone. Today, the concepts and language pioneered by Freud are openly used in the discussion of sexual problems. "Freud showed us we were not alone," says Father Ong. "We feel so close to one another that nobody has any secrets any more."

This common admission of sexuality ultimately finds expression in franker sex education courses in the Anaheim, Calif., and Evanston, Ill., school systems, in which grade-school children are encouraged to bring the whispered words of the playground into the classroom for open discussion. It permits the creation of special high schools for pregnant girls in San Francisco and New York. It enables both clerics and laymen within the Roman Catholic Church to challenge pastoral policy on celibacy and birth control. It even permits the manufacture of baby-boy dolls equipped with sex organs.

Appetites: The climate of candor in America

today is not, however, simply a matter of art and expression pushing forward to the applause of an increasingly tolerant public. There have always been writers like Havelock Ellis and D. H. Lawrence willing to talk frankly and an audience willing to listen. But, until recently, agencies of moral order like the church, the government, the family and the community have dictated what can and cannot be expressed in public. Since World War II, in America, however, these institutions have simply been overrun by the demands of a mass society that wants to see and hear everything.

Nowhere has this process been more graphically dramatized than in the erosion of film censorship. In the 1930s fear of government regulation drove Hollywood to create its own Production Code, which forbade a husband and wife to be shown in the same bed and banned the word buzzard because it sounded too much like bastard. The Roman Catholic Church also controlled film content through its Legion of Decency, whose "C" or "condemned" rating could bar a movie from hundreds of theaters fearful of local boycott.

After the second world war, however, both code and church censorship started to crack. In 1946, Howard Hughes released "The Outlaw" in the face of a "C" rating and culled a fortune on the strength of Jane Russell's titanic cleavage. Seven years later, when both the Legion and Hollywood refused to sanction "The Moon Is Blue" because of the word "virgin," producer Otto Preminger released it anyway and was amply reimbursed by the public. Again, in 1956, Preminger defied the code and its taboo on dope addiction when he released "The Man with the Golden Arm."

Feeble: Since then, the code has been revised twice, and the Legion of Decency has changed its name to the National Catholic Office for Motion Pictures and has liberalized its judgments. But the power

of both agencies is now feeble. Already this year five
major films have ignored a "C" rating, among them
"Blow-Up," "Reflections in a Golden Eye," and Preminger's "Hurry Sundown." "As far as I'm concerned
the public makes up its own mind," says the 73-year-old
chief executor of the Production Code, Geoffrey Shur-
lock. "America has in time grown up to accept sex.
All the taboos are beginning to break down, which is
probably the most healthy thing that could happen."
Adds Fordham's Father Culkin: "Now the media goes
directly to the public. The moralizers got so out of
touch, they shouted for so long, that after a while nobody listened."

The courts, the last official restraining arm of
society, have developed in recent cases such fluid guidelines for obscenity that local police agencies can seize
and prosecute only those films and books that are "utterly without socially redeeming value." "Censorship of
films and books has become simply a matter of taste,"
says veteran lawyer Ephraim London, an expert on
censorship who has argued a number of key cases before the Supreme Court. "Today there's absolutely
nothing you can't show or write about if it's done in
good taste, absolutely nothing. If the courts judge something obscene, they are in effect making an aesthetic
rather than a moral judgment. If the censorship rules
of 1950 were in effect today, two out of every three
films shown now would be banned." Even many of the
tasteless hard-core paperbacks which could, under the
law, be seized are more often than not ignored by district attorneys who feel no real pressure to do so from
the community.

Not only has the mass society acquired the muscle,
or perhaps more accurately, the money, to get what it
wants, but what it wants has changed as well, under
the pressure applied by a whole new generation of
young people. As Keith Richard, 23-year-old guitarist

with the Rolling Stones, proclaims: "We are not old men. We are not worried about petty morals." What the new generation wants is not simply bigger breasts and sexier scenes on wider screens. "They want to strip away all the sham and all the cant of their elders and to strive instead for truth and honesty," says TV impresario David Susskind. "This revolution has been made by young people and nothing will thwart it for the simple reason that truth will out. 'Tell it to me, baby. Tell it the way it really is.' These are the battle cries of the young."

Fashion designer Mary Quant, mother of the miniskirt, tells it as it is, or at least the way she sees it: "Am I the only woman who has ever wanted to go to bed with a man in the afternoon? Any law-abiding female, it used to be thought, waits until dark. Well, there are lots of girls who don't want to wait. Miniclothes are symbolic of them. So are cosmetics that seem natural and stay on right into bed and out again, because that's the point. All this decoration is put on in order to seduce a man to bed, so what's the sense of taking it all off?"

Metaphor: The shattering of taboos on language, fashion and manners generally is part of a larger disintegration of moral consensus in America. Vast numbers of Americans distrust their government. Catholics in increasing numbers simply ignore the church ban on birth control. The family has changed from a breeding ground of common values into a battleground of generations. These dislocations have moved many writers to reach for the strongest language in their arsenal to capture the chaos of their time. "We're in a time that's divorced from the past," says novelist Norman Mailer. "There's utterly no tradition anymore. It's a time when our nervous systems are being remade. There's an extraordinary amount of obscenity around—and it's in my new book. I had to write it that way despite the fact that I hate to add to all that obscenity." But such language, insists Mailer, "is the only metaphor to express the situation that produces Vietnam."

Things have changed radically since Mailer, in "The Naked and the Dead," had to invent the word "fug" to evoke the raw language of the American soldier in World War II. Today Mailer, Hubert Selby, and a whole school of new young novelists use obscenity not merely as an imitation of street speech but as an antidote to their own outrage and frustration at what they feel is the increasing dehumanization of the high-technology industrial state. "The real choice we have is not between dirty and not dirty," says Mailer. "It is between the creative artist, with his more or less corrupt soul, explaining life with his instinctive and curious gift for language, and the scientist, with his more or less corrupt soul, explaining life with his lenses, galvanometers and probes."

Mammal: Obscenity and nudity and eroticism, then, have become prime weapons for the artist as humanizer. He uses them to remind man that, amidst his electrical appliances and armaments and credit cards and daily costumes, he remains Homo sapiens. "Why don't we stop pretending that we're not mammals and that we don't do the things mammals do?" asks poet-playwright Michael McClure, author of "The Beard." "There's nothing new about my play. It could have been done 2,000 years ago." Man as mammal, sexual, innocent, is the theme of today's erotic painters who use nudity to affirm life.

"The nudity in all these things is very pure," explains 39-year-old Wynn Chamberlain, who paints his friends in open, smiling, superhygienic nudity. "There's been a great confusion in the public mind between prurient art and nude art. I never thought of my art as prurient—rather as subversive, wanting to shake up the world, to get people to loosen up and relax." Adds

Robert Rosinek, 31, who turns the sex act into an aesthetic matching of pure colors and forms: "I've taken sex back to the Garden of Eden. Sex shouldn't be this commercial, mechanical, jaded thing. I use the canvas as I use an empty bed. I try to create something beautiful in both."

Costume: In much the same spirit, the dancers of Ann Halprin's Dancers' Workshop in San Francisco create nude ballets designed to help liberate their emotions and conquer the audience's fear of the human body. "The human body is just another costume," says Mrs. Halprin. "Nudity is just part of a new way of being able to express feelings." This, in a sense, is the feeling of most artists, that nudity and sexuality must be faced and accepted by society as part of a general confrontation of life. Once the artist has created this mature audience, he can move on to more important matters. "You have to get to the point where people aren't shocked any more," says Ed Sanders, underground editor and lead singer with The Fugs, a scatological rock group. "It's not being jaded—it's when people know sex is not a threat to them and they accept it."

For Terry Southern, black-humorist, author of "Candy" and the screenwriter of "Barbarella," at least part of the battle is already over. "If you're writing about longshoremen," he says, "you can finally put down how they really talk and get it published. It's a nice thing to have over with, a kind of purging. Now a writer doesn't have to use those words again. He might, but he doesn't *have* to. As long as the old taboos existed, you felt you had to use them or you'd be selling out. It was all a big drag."

Inevitably, freedom of expression in an open society is as accessible to the smutmaster as to the serious artist. If the new candor has strengthened the writing of America's best novelists, it has merely polluted the pulp literature that sells to millions. Many best sellers simply pander perversions and profanity for profit. "These books aren't written, they're manufactured by formula," says Bennett Cerf, head of Random House and a pioneer in the publication of "Ulysses." "They set up a list of perversions and throw them in at 30-page intervals."

Gasp: The purveyors of this soft-core pornography legitimize their ventures with the same rationale used by serious artists: that they are breaking the bonds of puritan society and helping America to grow up. "Bernard Geis Associates is working toward a better, healthier, saner society," says Bernard Geis, publisher of "Valley of the Dolls," which chronicled the sexual aberrations of show-business figures, and "The Exhibitionist," just released, which salivates over the unhappy sex life of a Hollywood starlet. "We are working toward the last gasp. We will publish a book that will make the public gasp for the last time. When we do, we will have reached a more adult civilization." But, says David Slavitt, a poet and former *Newsweek* film critic who wrote "The Exhibitionist" under the nom de plume of Henry Sutton: "If pure pornography sold as well as the stuff I'm writing, Mr. Geis would sell pornography. After all, he's a businessman."

So is Radley Metzger, whose early career as a "serious" filmmaker left him broke until he formed Audubon Films, which makes and distributes "exploitation" movies all over the world. He has already grossed $1.5 million as the distributor of "I, a Woman," and will make more from his own "Carmen, Baby," a glossy but tawdry version of Mérimée in modern undress. Metzger's defense of the exploitation film is nothing if not logical: "If people think there is too much eroticism in motion pictures, what brought them there in the first place?" Metzger has found, as did *Playboy* publisher Hugh Hefner, that there is a vast and variegated audience waiting to be titillated. "Why are laughter, anger

or pity legitimate reactions, but not sexual excitement?''
asks Hefner.

Playboy is expected to reach the 5 million mark in
circulation this year. Audubon is planning more expensive films aimed at a broader audience, and American International, in Hollywood, which has made its
fortune on such variations on sex, violence, motor-
cycles and mayhem as "The Wild Angels," "Riot on
Sunset Strip" and "How to Stuff a Wild Bikini," will
launch its biggest production yet—$1.5 million—next
spring. "These best sellers and films are vulgar," comments lawyer Ephraim London. "But they are no more
vulgar than our architecture and neon strips and the
pink flamingos on our lawns. Why should our best-
selling films and books be any exception to a general
vulgarity?"

Still, the force of this logic does not stop citizens
like London himself from worrying about the impact
of distorted images of sex upon children. In fact, the
new candor in the arts does not horrify parents as much
as it bewilders them, forcing them to reassess their role
as moral arbiter for their family. Some parents simply
put their faith in the good judgment of their children,
like the mother of two teen-age girls in Atlanta who
says: "If something is cheap, they can recognize it for
the trash it is." But some parents are determined to stem
the tide, like Ruth Vaulman, a Chicago housewife with
five children who recently led a letter-writing and telephone campaign against a local showing of "I, a
Woman." "Someone reminded me that Adam was
nude. But Adam didn't go dancing across my neighborhood screen. Everything is just sex, sex, sex," says
Mrs. Vaulman. "We mothers are concerned and don't
know what to do."

Smut: They are not alone in their concern.
Twenty-three separate bills on obscenity have already
been introduced into the 90th Congress. One, which

establishes a Presidential commission on obscenity and pornography, passed this year after eight years of effort by South Dakota's Sen. Karl Mundt. The commission, to be composed of eighteen citizens appointed by the President, will spend up to $75 a day studying dirty books, working out a fresh definition of pornography and investigating the sale and distribution of smut with a view to proposing new legislation for its control. The commission has stirred very little enthusiasm in Washington. Most officials agree with the U.S. Post Office's general counsel Timothy May. "Sex is troubling for society, but government ought to stay out of it," he says, "unless there is widespread licentiousness which becomes harmful. The government is not here to enforce the Ten Commandments, and the wants of society are generally twenty years ahead of government."

Even the most powerful agent of moral restraint, the Catholic Church, has been struggling not to suppress the new candor but to develop a more flexible attitude itself in an effort to remain relevant within the permissive society. While conservative clerics in Rome, like Cardinal Alfredo Ottaviani, deplore the relaxation of mores in the West, more "progressive" prelates urge a liberalization of the traditional Catholic position on sex and sin. "A lot of religious people realize that the Carrie Nation approach to obscenity is no longer the style of our life," says Father John Reedy, editor of *Ave Maria* magazine, one of a number of Catholic journals pressing for change. "Today's attitude is to appeal to the individual as an adult."

In fact, much of the new candor is coming from dissident Catholics themselves, among them the growing number of priests who are openly attacking the church policy on celibacy. One, James Kavanaugh, author of "A Modern Priest Looks at His Outdated Church," has left the church, but his attacks continue. "The church cannot subdivide the moral law into tiny absolutes," he says. "It cannot make God into a crotchety old lady with frayed nerves. The church's distorted image of man's weakness and inclination to sin prevents it from serving the people." "Religion has been used to cover up things," comments Lutheran theologian Martin E. Marty. "Some churchmen have simply said 'We are sick and tired of it.' They'll grab all kinds of instruments to change it—the most evocative tools at hand, both literary and linguistic."

Shape: In any case, no action, by either church or state, is likely to impede the advance of the permissive society. Already rumbles from other Western countries suggest the shape of things to come in America. Recently, in Holland, a nude girl appeared on Dutch national television with only a newspaper occasionally between her and the camera; there was no great public outcry. A new Swedish film, "I'm Curious," shows what one observer called "an animated Nordic version of the Kama Sutra," with four explicit scenes of lovemaking. In America, Terry Southern is at work on a novel that explores the possibility of producing "artistic" pornographic films for profit. And French director Roger Vadim in "Barbarella" presents not only his wife, Jane Fonda, in the nude, but a glimpse of the year 40,000 in which, as he explains it, "there are no taboos on sex, eroticism or nudity, no sin in nudity or the sex act."

Vadim's vision of the earth as a great pleasure dome is as speculative as anyone else's. But it does raise the crucial question of where the new permissiveness is leading, whether the breakdown of the old order is going to lead to some new moral system or whether it is simply going to lead to the progressive discarding of all social restraint. Some artists and critics feel it is not going to lead anywhere, that it is simply one more swing in the pendulum of history between Dionysian

and Apollonian styles of behavior. "I would expect the
pendulum to swing back," says British director Tony
Richardson. "Another historical movement will occur,
some major cataclysm, and society will need heroics,
more codes, ideals. All victories are limited; they are
never total. Just when you think you have advanced
for all time, you find you are mistaken."

Architect and cosmic thinker Buckminster Fuller
believes the pendulum is swinging back already—not
the pendulum of history, but of evolution. As Fuller
sees it, man's role as a procreator in an advanced society diminishes as fewer and fewer offspring are
needed to ensure the survival of the species. "In the
days of baby-making," he says, "the forbidden areas
of the body were kept secret and promising in order to
make us look forward to getting into bed. Once we
start exposing ourselves as we're doing, sex gets to be a
bore. The sexes themselves start to blur, and homosexuality increases, which also cuts down babies. Nature is putting on the brakes and man is unconsciously
following. This is really an anti-erotic and anti-sexual
trend."

Most social thinkers, however, are unwilling to
accept the dictates either of history or evolution, believing that man still exerts a crucial control over the
shape of his future. They see the tumbling of the old
codes not as the beginning of a moral decline, but as
the beginning of a search for new values. If society
does collapse in a hedonistic frenzy, it will be because
this search has failed. "I think it's good to have an
expressive, free and imaginative society," says Max
Lerner, "as long as you recognize some limits. These
limits don't have to be puritanical. Without limits, our
society can become as hedonistic as the world of the
Marquis de Sade—going toward the most sadistic and
primitive drives in the human being. It's not enough to

break things down. Such a trend is not ultimately satis-
fying in itself. New values must be found and I believe
young people are trying to find these values. That's
where I place my hope.''

DRUGS AND YOUR CHILD

BY DONALD ZOCHERT

Marijuana is the one "mind-expanding" drug most widely used by college and high school students.

It is the easiest to obtain.

It is the cheapest to buy.

And it is, in the opinion of many physicians and psychologists, who have worked most closely with it, the least dangerous.

This is a new look at an old weed.

It is not an apologia for marijuana, but an attempt to look at some opinions and research that often have been obscured in the faddish and fearful obsession with the drug scene.

The first section represents the view of Dr. Roswell D. Johnson, a former pediatrician who has been director of University Health Services at Brown University since 1963. His remarks were made last fall at a meeting of the National Assn. of College Admissions Counselors.

Donald Zochert is a staff writer for the Chicago Daily News.

This article was one in a series that appeared in the Chicago Daily News *(March 1969) and is reprinted with permission from the* Chicago Daily News.

Dr. Helen H. Nowlis, whose views are presented in the second section, is professor of psychology and research consultant on student affairs at the University of Rochester. She directed the Drug Education Project for the National Assn. of Student Personnel Administrators under contract to the U.S. Food and Drug Administration.

Her remarks were made last week in Chicago at the 24th National Conference on Higher Education.

The final section presents the results of what has been called the first carefully controlled attempt to study the clinical and psychological effects of marijuana.

Dr. Johnson's findings:

Typical 'pothead' a rarity: Johnson

"In our frame of reference we need to know how many students use drugs—how often they use them and what they use. Unfortunately, there are precious few studies that give us any reliable figures.

"Informal but independent studies concerning marijuana on our campus suggest that close to 40 per cent of the students have had experience with it at some time. This, of course, does not mean that 40 per cent are now using it.

"As far as we can tell some 8 to 10 per cent are still occasional users but a typical 'pothead' for whom the use of marijuana has become a way of life is indeed a rarity.

"It is generally agreed that the drug that has caused more trouble than all the others combined is alcohol.

"Last year alone on our campus this caused broken arms, broken legs, broken backs and fractured skulls from falls; broken hands from fights; severed arteries from putting a fist through a glass door or window, and death from driving at turnpike speeds down a city street with subsequent loss of control. . . .

"Space does not permit elaboration on the cigaret problem, so severely pinpointed by the surgeon general's office as a clearcut cause of death and disability —a claim never made by the same group against marijuana. . . .

"From the point of view of the concerns that you and I share, marijuana's greatest hazard is that it may become a way of life.

"It does not produce the same type of hangover that alcohol does. It produces an elevation of mood with diminution of cares and induces a passivity that many students find highly pleasing.

"The passivity is the effect that is incompatible with academic production. The passivity, likewise, is the very factor that makes crimes of violence and sex outrages uncommon. . . .

"I find it difficult to assess cause and effect in the students who are 'dropping out' and using marijuana. Critics of drug use, I'm afraid, are too prone to attribute it to the drug.

"This is frequently true, but it is naive to feel that it is always that simple.

"I've seen very few students who used marijuana for fun wind up as a dropout, unless he already had the despair and the alienation that characterizes that particular syndrome. . . .

"Another problem I am facing, which also has been manmade, is the magnification of the dangers of marijuana with the result that when one tries to talk about the more dangerous hallucinogens and amphetamines, young people from grade school up simply will not buy it. . . .

"Too many young people have used marijuana,

too many have seen others use it and too many have seen it cause less havoc than alcohol to buy all the scare stories.

"Most of them have not seen bad LSD 'trips' or reactions, they have not seen a shaky, scrawny 'speed' freak, so they put all of our dire warnings in the same bag and refuse to believe us when we say that those drugs are 'different.'

"Exaggeration of the marijuana hazard is either intentional or attributal to a lack of knowledge. It is not only fundamentally dishonest but it is a serious practical hazard.

"I think marijuana is a dangerous drug and should be so treated. Any substance that reduces man's rationality is suspect, be it the exotic drugs or alcohol.

"Any substance that can cause cancer is also suspect, but how hard we sit on the panic button depends on whose ox is being gored."

Little scientific knowledge: Nowlis

Views of Dr. Nowlis:

"Before beginning our discussion of marijuana, it should be pointed out that it is a drug only by virtue of its being so labeled in the Marijuana Tax Act of 1937 and subsequent legislation.

"Marijuana is one of several names for a plant, Cannabis sativa.

"It is no more a drug than tea leaves or coffee beans are drugs. All do, however, contain varying substances that are drugs. . . .

"As is true of virtually all drugs, its (marijuana's) use may result in adverse effects at some dosage level in some people under some circumstances, some patterns of use or reasons for use. . . .

"Despite the fact that cannibas, in one form or another, has been used for thousands of years in many parts of the world, we have amazingly little scientific knowledge about it.

"Marijuana is one substance about which everyone seems to have an opinion or belief and about which all kinds of people have written, often with more passion than knowledge.

"Most scientists . . . generally agree, sometimes reluctantly, that there is no good evidence that the relatively low-potency marijuana normally available in this country is physically or psychologically harmful for most people when smoked occasionally or even fairly regularly over a relatively short period of months or even several years.

"On the other hand, there is no good evidence that chronic use of such relatively low potency marijuana over long periods is not harmful.

"That research simply has not been done. . . .

"Testimony presented before the Senate Subcommittee on Juvenile Delinquency in March, 1968, by Dr. Stanley F. Yolles, Director of the National Institute of Health, represents the worst one can honestly say about marijuana:

"With regard to the hazards of marijuana, the evidence is less clear. Clinicians have reported occasional panic reactions resulting from marijuana usage —especially in the novice. The frequency of these episodes has not been determined in this country but is believed to be rare. . . .

" 'With regard to long-term hazards of marijuana, accepted scientific evidence is minimal. . . . In general, most investigators in the United States have agreed with the findings of the so-called LaGuardia Report, which failed to find evidence to support charges of severe personality change resulting from marijuana usage.

" 'Additionally, the argument that marijuana usage leads over time to heroin usage has been seriously questioned by Dr. Halbach of the World Health Organization who notes no pharmacological link between cannabis and opiates.

" 'His hypothesis has been supported by the President's Crime Commission Task Force on Drugs and other groups.'

"There are a number of other questions that deserve careful consideration as we assess the current legal status of marijuana. . . . How effective are current laws in accomplishing their stated purpose?

"If the criterion for effectiveness . . . is reduction in the use of marijuana, the answer must be a resounding 'No.' Estimates of use vary from 2,000,000 to 20,000,000.

"No one really knows, chiefly because it is impossible to get accurate information about anything which involves admitting to the commission of a felony.

"There is little question, however, that there has been a sharp and dramatic increase within the last two to three years. . . . This has occurred in the face of penalties in many cases more harsh than those for crimes of violence. . . .

"An increasing number of people . . . are deeply disturbed by the impact of these particular laws on the attitude of many young people toward the law in general.

"If I were asked to designate the greater evil, current use of marijuana or the impact of drug laws on the attitude of young people toward law, I would without question name the latter.

"Once having broken a major law and, whether apprehended or not, having been labeled a criminal, it is less difficult to break other laws when another issue arises.

"The wheeling and dealing that goes on when, as is the case in some states, the laws are so absurd that no attorney wants to prosecute, no jury wants to con-

vict and no judge wants to sentence, particularly when
sentences are mandatory, creates more disrespect for
the law than can be tolerated if we are to be a society
governed by law."

Chronic users, nonusers tested

What has been described as "the first carefully
controlled attempt to study the clinical and psychological effects of smoking marijuana was conducted at
the Boston University School of Medicine.

The results of the experiment were reported in the
current *Scientific American,* a recent issue of *Science,*
and the *Chicago Daily News* last December.

Two groups of young men were involved in the
experiment. One was composed of nine men who smoked
cigarets but had never smoked marijuana. The other
included eight chronic users of marijuana.

The subjects went through three laboratory sessions, smoking three different kinds of cigarets: one
with a high dose of marijuana, one with a low dose,
and one with only tobacco.

The chronic users went through one session, smoking the cigarets with high doses of marijuana.

At no time did the volunteers know which of the
three kinds of cigaret they were smoking.

There were these results:

The volunteers who had never smoked marijuana
were unable to tell the high-dose cigaret from the low
dose. Their performance on a written test and a test of
coordination, however, dropped sharply after smoking marijuana.

The chronic users of marijuana got "high" on
their marijuana cigarets. Their performance on the two
laboratory tests, however, either remained the same or
improved.

The volunteers experienced some distortion of

time, a little emphoria and no visual or hearing distortions. All effects had vanished after two hours.

No reaction to marijuana smoking was as severe as that experienced by five potential volunteers to the nicotine in regular cigarets during a practice session. These prospective subjects became dizzy, turned pale and got sweaty palms.

The researchers concluded that marijuana is a "relatively mild intoxicant," which acts upon the higher centers of the brain—thinking and mood, rather than reflexes and coordination—and with minor, short-lived, aftereffects.

Specific problems must be probed

Nearly every professional who has worked with the problem of youth and drugs has complained that the effort expended on research into the pharmacology and effects of these "mind-changers" has been woefully inadequate.

The Boston University study is important not because it "proves" anything about marijuana, but because it is an attempt to understand it scientifically.

It is important also to understand marijuana psychologically and socially, to seek out voices of authority and reasonableness in a phenomenon marked by established misconceptions and occasional hysteria.

In his testimony before the Senate subcommittee on Juvenile Delinquincy last spring, Dr. Stanley Yolles identified what he felt to be the "critical" issue of the drug scene.

"In trying to understand scientifically the problem of drug abuse," he said, "one must look beyond the specific problems of such agents as LSD, marijuana, amphetamines, and barbiturates to some of the underlying causes of widespread drug use and abuse.

"If we are to get to the root of the problem, we must be prepared to investigate and identify the underlying problems which lead people to choose to distort or ward off reality with drugs."

BEFORE YOUR KID TRIES DRUGS

BY STANLEY YOLLES

Until quite recently, most parents of teen-agers were not especially concerned with facts about drug abuse. The use and misuse of new and ancient mind-altering preparations were largely matters of medical, pharmaceutical and, as regards control, legal interest. Any compendium on "what every parent should know" might comfortably exclude the subject.

No longer. Today our pill-oriented society is alarmed and confused over the growing abuse of drugs among young people. Waves of shock follow in the wake of reports of campus-wide pot. The word "marijuana" has, like it or not, infiltrated the nation's playgrounds.

And the problem is real. Drugs such as marijuana, the amphetamines, the barbiturates, the opiates, and LSD have become pot, speed, bennies, goofballs, junk, and acid in the world of youth whose innocence fre-

Stanley F. Yolles, M.D., is director of the National Institute of Mental Health.

This article first appeared in the New York Times *magazine (Nov. 17, 1968) © 1969/1968 The New York Times Company and is reprinted here by permission.*

quently blurs the distinction between being turned-on and turned-off.

As adults whose lives may include some acquaintance with drugs, such as alcohol, tranquilizers and other pills, we naturally desire to protect those who are too young to make mature and informed decisions. The issues surrounding the use of dangerous drugs are many. Not the least of these is the law. The law-breaking use of illicit drugs can jeopardize not only health but the pursuit of careers. And for those youngsters whose curiosity may lead from experiment to regular use of mind-affecting chemicals, there are the potential threats of stunted development and alienation.

Fortunately, there is some evidence that the "Now Generation" holds a healthy respect for the facts and for the findings of science. While parental panic and admonition are little value as guidance and tend to stoke the fires of adolescent rebellion, knowledge of the facts may help. The current wane in the use of LSD, for example, may be traced at least in part to the reported possibility of genetic damage.

As the principal Federal agency responsible for stimulating research on drug abuse, the National Institute of Mental Health is vitally interested in strengthening our arsenal of knowledge and in helping to make the facts available to the public. Recently, the Institute published a series of leaflets which are being distributed widely throughout the country. They attempt to answer some of the most frequently asked questions surrounding the use of marijuana, LSD, narcotics, barbiturates and amphetamines. Here are some of the points about drugs made in the N.I.M.H. booklets:

LSD: A powerful man-made chemical, lysergic acid diethylamide, generally called LSD, was first developed in 1938 from ergot alkaloids. A single ounce is enough to provide 300,000 of the usual doses. A mind-altering drug, LSD is legally classed as an hallucinogen, as are peyote, mescaline, psilocybin, DMT and STP. LSD is used legally only for controlled research purposes. It is illicitly produced in makeshift laboratories. Users refer it to as "acid."

An average dose of LSD, amounting to a speck, has effects that last from 8 to 10 hours. Users take it in a sugar cube, on a cracker, on a cookie or can lick it off a stamp or other impregnated object. The drug increases the pulse and heart rate, causes a rise in blood pressure and temperature, dilated eye pupils, shaking of the hands and feet, cold sweaty palms, a flushed face or paleness, shivering, chills with goose-pimples, a wet mouth, irregular breathing, nausea, loss of appetite, and distortion of the physical senses.

People who use LSD report a number of effects. The first effects, they indicate, are likely to be sudden changes in their physical senses. Walls may appear to move, colors seem stronger and more brilliant. They "see" unusual patterns unfolding before them. Flat objects seem to become three-dimensional. Taste, smell, hearing and touch seem more acute. One sensory impression may be translated or merged into another: music may appear as a color, and colors seem to possess taste.

A confusing yet common reaction among users is the simultaneous experience of strong, opposite emotions; they may feel simultaneously happy and sad, depressed and elated, or relaxed and tense. They report sensations of losing the normal feeling of boundaries between body and space and get the notion they can float or fly. Effects can be different at different times in the same individual. Responses, even in carefully controlled studies, cannot be predicted. For this reason, users refer to "good trips," or "bad trips," to describe their experience.

The LSD user loses his sense of time, though he may remain conscious. He is able to reason logically, up to a point, and usually remembers the effects after the drug wears off. He may report, for example, the fascination he felt over an object such as a chair or a vase. On larger doses, he may feel mystical and report a sense of rebirth or fresh insight. Studies fail to support the theory that LSD increases creativity.

Hospital studies report the following reactions: Panic—the user grows frightened because he cannot stop the drug's action, and he fears he is losing his mind. Paranoia—he becomes increasingly suspicious, feeling that someone is trying to harm him or control his thinking. This feeling may last some 70 hours after the drug has worn off. Recurrence (also known as "flashbacks")—days, weeks, or months after LSD use is stopped, sights and sensations may recur.

Long-lasting mental illness may result if a non-medically supervised experience becomes acutely disturbing. The strange sensations and clash of moods caused by the drug can be overwhelming even for a mature person. For young people who are undergoing emotional development and transition, the effects can be even more frightening.

Just how LSD works in the body is not yet known. But it seems to affect the levels of certain chemicals in the brain and to produce changes in the brain's electrical activity. Animal experiments suggest that the brain's normal filtering and screening out process becomes blocked, causing it to become flooded with unselected sights and sounds. Studies of chronic users indicate that they may continue to suffer from an overload of stimulation to their senses. Frequently, effects recur months after the drug is discontinued.

Long-term effects of LSD use are under close investigation. Short-term or immediate dangers include the user's sensation that he can fly or float with ease, and that he is invincible. Accidental deaths have been reported. Users who suffer "bad trips" undergo temporary or longer-lasting psychosis. Chromosomal changes observed in LSD users have raised concern among scientists that these breaks may cause birth defects in the offspring of users.

Marijuana: A drug found in the flowering tops and leaves of the Indian hemp plant, *cannabis sativa*, marijuana grows in mild climates in countries around the world. The leaves and flowers of the plant are dried and crushed or chopped into small pieces and smoked in short cigarettes or pipes. It can be sniffed or taken in food. The cigarettes are commonly known as reefers, joints, and sticks. The smoke is harsh, and smells like burnt rope or dried grasses, with a sweetish odor. Its use is restricted and subject throughout the world to legal sanctions. There is no known medical use for marijuana. Pot, tea, grass, weed, Mary Jane, hash and kif are all names for marijuana.

The long-term physical effects are not yet known. The drug cannot yet, therefore, be considered medically safe. The research needed to weigh the effects of chronic use is in its earliest stages. Recent synthesis of the drug's active ingredient, *tetrahydrocannabinol*, now permits such investigation. The more obvious physical reactions include rapid heart beat, lowering of body temperature, and reddening of the eyes. The drug also changes blood sugar levels, stimulates the appetite, and dehydrates the body.

Effects on the emotions and senses vary widely, depending on the amount and strength of the marijuana used. The social setting in which it is taken and what the user expects also influence his reaction to the drug. Usually, the effect is felt quickly, in about 15 minutes after inhaling the smoke of the cigarette, and can last from 2 to 4 hours. Reactions range from depression to a feeling of excitement. Some users, however, experience no change of mood at all.

Sense of time and distance frequently becomes distorted. A minute may seem like an hour. Something near may seem far away. Any task or decision requiring good reflexes and clear thinking is affected by the drug. For this reason, driving is dangerous while under its influence. One of the more subtle results of regular marijuana use by young people lies in its influence on their personality growth and development—something that we have not determined as yet. Scientific findings, however, seem to point to rather deleterious effects.

Some investigators challenge the common belief that the drug is innocuous. In a survey reported in Boston last May, a group of West Coast researchers found that among 2,700 practicing mental health professionals, 1,887 patients with adverse reactions to marijuana were seen over a period of 18 months. At the same professional meeting, two researchers studying the "behavioral toxicity" of marijuana reported that their preliminary findings indicated that it may not be the "benign euphoriant" commonly alleged. Dr. Lincoln D. Clark and Edwin N. Nakashima of the University of Utah held that ". . . the very unpredictability of marijuana on different individuals and on the same individual at different times and under different conditions increases the risk to the user."

Stimulant Drugs: Amphetamines, first produced in the 1920's for medical use, are stimulants to the central nervous system. Best known for the ability to combat fatigue and sleepiness, they are also sometimes used to curb appetite. Under the supervision of a physician they may be used legally for medical purposes. The most commonly abused stimulants are Benzedrine, Dexedrine and Methedrine. Pep pills, bennies and speed are common names.

These drugs Methedrine and Dexedrine, do not produce physical dependence. The body does, however, develop a tolerance which requires increasingly large doses. They increase the heart rate, raise the blood pressure, cause palpitations, dilate the pupils and cause dry mouth, sweating, headache, diarrhea and paleness. Action of the heart and metabolism is speeded up through stimulation of the release of *norepinephrine*, a substance stored in nerve endings, which then becomes concentrated in the higher centers of the brain. Exhaustion and temporary psychosis, which may result from abuse of stimulants, may require hospitalization.

The injection of Methedrine into a vein, a highly dangerous practice known as "speeding," has aroused medical authorities. "Speeding" may result in critical serum hepatitis. When injected in unaccustomed high doses, the drug can cause death.

Used without medical prescription, for kicks or staying awake for long periods, these drugs can drive a person to do things beyond his physical endurance that leave him exhausted. Heavy doses may cause a temporary toxic psychosis (mental derangement) requiring hospitalization. This is usually accompanied by auditory and visual hallucinations. Abrupt withdrawal after heavy abuse can result in deep and suicidal depression. Long-term heavy users are usually irritable, unstable and, like other chronic drug abusers, show social, intellectual and emotional breakdown.

Sedatives: These belong to a large family of drugs which relax the nervous system. The best known are the barbiturates, first produced in 1846, from barbituric acid. They range from the short-acting, fast-starting pentobarbital (Nembutal) and secobarbital (Seconal) to the long-acting, slow-starting phenobarbital (Luminol), amobarbital (Amytal) and butabarbital (Butisol). The short-acting preparations are the ones most commonly abused. They are called barbs and goofballs.

Taken in normal, medically supervised doses, barbiturates mildly depress the action of the nerves, skeletal muscles and the heart muscle. They slow down the heart rate and breathing, and lower the blood pressure. In higher doses, the effects resemble alcoholic drunkenness: confusion, slurred speech, staggering and deep sleep. These drugs produce physical dependence. Body tolerance to them requires increasingly higher doses.

If the drug is withdrawn abruptly, the user suffers withdrawal sickness with cramps, nausea, dilirium and convulsions, and in some cases, sudden death. Withdrawal must take place in a hospital over a period of several weeks on gradually reduced doses.

Large doses are potentially lethal. Any dosage may cause accidents because perception of objects becomes distorted, reactions and response are slowed. Barbiturates are a leading cause of automobile accidents, especially when taken with alcohol. Users may react to the drug more strongly at one time than at another. They may become confused about how many pills they have taken, and die of an accidental overdose. Barbiturates are a leading cause of accidental poison deaths in the United States, and frequently implicated in suicides.

Narcotics: The term narcotics refers, generally, to opium and painkilling drugs made from opium, such as heroin, morphine, methadone and codeine. These are other opiates are obtained from the juice of the poppy fruit. Several synthetic drugs, such as demerol and nalorphine, are also classed as narcotics. Cocaine, made from cocoa leaves, and marijuana are classed legally but not chemically as narcotic drugs. Heroin is the narcotic most used by today's addicts. It is often called junk, H, snow, stuff or smack.

Heroin depresses certain areas of the brain and other parts of the nervous system. It reduces hunger, thirst, the sex drive and feelings of pain. When a person addicted to heroin stops the drug, withdrawal sickness sets in. He may sweat, shake, get chills, diarrhea, nausea and suffer sharp abdominal and leg cramps. Recent findings show that the body's physical dependence on heroin lasts much longer than previously thought. Unexpectedly pure or large doses can and do result in death.

Typically, the first emotional reaction to heroin is an easing of fear and a relief from worry. Feeling "high" may be followed by a period of inactivity bordering on stupor. The drug appears to dull the edges of reality. Addicts have reported that heroin "makes my troubles roll off my mind," and "it makes me feel more sure of myself."

While medical treatments have been established to cure physical dependence on the drug, psychological dependence on heroin as a way to escape facing life may take extended rehabilitation.

The term "addiction" is most commonly applied to the abuse of heroin and other opiates. Authorities now think in terms of drug "dependence" rather than addiction. Dependence can be physical or psychological —or both. With true narcotics, the abuser suffers both. He is hooked as his body becomes physically dependent on the drug. Further, his body grows tolerant to the drug, which means that repeated and larger doses are required to achieve the same effects.

One of the points made to parents by pot-smoking youngsters concerns adult use of alcohol. "Well, you drink, don't you?" they are wont to respond, thrusting home with all the thrill of a newly discovered challenge. The analogy is pale. In the first place, the use of alcoholic beverages by persons over 21 is not against the law. Secondly, the immoderate use of alcohol as a crutch by some people does nothing to recommend this or other chemical means of "copping out." To the contrary, problem drinking and alcoholism are currently subjects of intensive medical and social research.

Thirdly, the acceptability of moderate social drinking assumes that adults are mature enough to make mature decisions as to their behavior. And finally, there is the irrefutable fact that the fresh young years of personality growth and development are dangerously inappropriate for any chemical means of confounding reality.

As authorities well recognize, neither laws nor awareness of the medical facts can themselves secure drug abuse prevention. Nor can we stop people from using alcohol or cigarettes as support or as a bandage for their psychic wounds. Ours is a drug-oriented culture. From aspirin to sleeping pills, from tranquilizers to the "pill," Americans of all ages are ingesting drugs in greater variety and greater number than ever before.

It is not so much the phenomenon of use, however, but the mis-use and abuse of drugs that bears close investigation. Why do people choose to distort or to ward off reality through chemical means? Perhaps we deal with deep-rooted feelings of alienation. Alienation among the young has been characterized as "rebellion without a cause . . . rejection without a program . . . a refusal of what is without a vision of what should be." As scientists, we are left to probe whatever reasons can be found for this sad anomaly.

UNDERSTANDING SEX IN THE AGE OF THE PILL

BY GORDON CLANTON

The church of Jesus Christ stands at the threshold of total irrelevance vis-à-vis one of man's most pressing concerns—his sexuality and the religious and societal demands associated with it. Although our people live in the age of Kinsey, Hefner and Enovid, the church and its spokesmen continue the futile attempt to extrapolate a full understanding of sex from the thought of Moses, Augustine and Calvin. In so doing we pretend that nothing has changed, that the old answers are adequate for new questions, that an absolutist ethical code can serve men's needs in the midst of unprecedented change.

It is not the intention of this essay to suggest that because behavior patterns are changing the church must change. I am calling not for accommodationism but for a creative and prophetic confrontation with the

Mr. Clanton, a minister of the Presbyterian Church, U.S., is engaged in Ph.D. studies in religion and society at the Graduate Theological Union, Berkeley, California.

This article first appeared in the January 8, 1969 issue of The Christian Century, *copyright 1969, Christian Century Foundation. Reprinted by permission.*

situation of modern man and a consideration of the possibility that an honest appropriation of the gospel to our changing times might actually produce some new religious and social norms.

The paramount change we must deal with is the advent of the oral contraceptive—the Pill. The Pill has joined certain breakthroughs in education and medicine and the increasing anonymity of urban life in a frontal assault on those reasons for sexual abstinence upon which the church has depended for so long—infection, detection and conception.

Of course, it may be argued that the Pill is not 100 per cent effective. But such an argument avoids the point. The odds with the Pill are very good—so good that our society has in fact embraced the Pill as the basis for substantial changes in behavior. Indeed, a gynecologist I know offers this evidence of public acceptance of the oral contraceptive: more than half of the unmarried coeds in our larger universities are taking the Pill. And, of course, science promises a more effective pill, once-a-month pills, morning-after pills, mass temporary sterilization via treated water supplies, and so on.

The church must assume the effectiveness of the Pill or fall even *further* behind. At the very least we must assume that the people to whom we churchmen minister have assumed its effectiveness. If the church ignores the Pill's impact it may soon find that it has the attention only of those who do not want to make use of the Pill or who have real reservations about its effectiveness. The church must face this fact: the people endorse the Pill and because they do their demands on their pastors are different from those of the Pre-Pill Age.

The growing irrelevance of the church in relation to sex has spawned a host of tragic absurdities in our religious and social values. For example, because the church has insisted that virginity is the only acceptable condition for an unmarried Christian, we have failed to provide any moral guidance at all for the Christian young people who become sexually involved before marriage—and *that* means that we have nothing to say to one of the most important concerns of perhaps half of our young people. The church must acknowledge that unmarried, sexually experienced Christians really do exist, and must extend a constructive ministry to them.

Another absurdity generated by our irrelevance is "technical virginity." The proper and blessed estate is defined in terms of an intact hymen. Hence young couples sleep together nude, take showers together, experiment dangerously with mutual masturbation and partial insertions—all while subjecting themselves to considerable strain and piling up burdens of guilt which may hamper full enjoyment of sex as a part of marriage. And when it is all over they are able to congratulate themselves on having been very moral because no membrane was broken.

Rather than continue to document the obvious with an endless parade of our society's sexual neuroses, I turn to two basic errors which the church and church people have made in regard to sex.

(1) In the first place, we have tended to insist that religious, legal and personal standards must be the same. That is to say, the church has held that one rather narrow code of sexual behavior is taught by Scripture and therefore must be taught by the church, that the same code should be enforced by the civil government (on *all* citizens—not just on Christians) and that the personal standards of each individual must conform precisely to these religious and legal norms. As a result our society must bear the burden of hundreds of laws of rather dubious value prohibiting fornication, adultery, homosexuality, sodomy, exhibitionism and so

on—and to add to the confusion these laws vary remarkably from state to state. Attempts at reform are difficult because of the tendency to demand uniformity of religious, legal and personal standards. Hence a state senator who favors repeal of a law which allows a man to be imprisoned for 20 years for having an "unnatural relationship" with a goat is attacked by defenders of "Christian morality" as one who condones —or perhaps indulges in—such practices. Even were it desirable to do so, such laws cannot control behavior. Such laws impose "Christian standards" on a pluralistic society and make a mockery of the individual freedom implied in the gospel. The church must learn to demand legislation only when all members of the society will benefit from it. No one has the right to demand statutory codification of his own personal morality.

(2) The church's second major error in its attempt to deal with sex is its insistence that total abstinence is the only moral possibility for the unmarried Christian. It has been held that to discuss ways in which one might apply the gospel in his use of nonmarital sex would be to give the church's approval to nonmarital sex. Instead we leave our young people without guidance while pretending that such guidance is unnecessary. It is as though driver education teachers were to stop instructing young drivers how to deal with dangerous skids "because careful drivers never have skids." The church seeking to witness in the Age of the Pill must confront the fact that many Christian young people are sexually involved and must attempt to provide them with some relevant guidance beyond the most common piece of counsel—i.e., "DON'T!" If we churchmen do not rise to this challenge we shall convince our youth that we stand ready to help them only with peripheral matters. Then the already large number of young people who feel they cannot talk with their pastors about sex will increase.

In light of these problems the church should begin at once a process which might be called the demythologization of sex; that is, we must begin to teach that sex itself is morally neutral. In the Age of the Pill, sex outside of marriage need not result in social disgrace, syphilis or pregnancy. Sex, like chess, conversation and the stock market, is, in and of itself, morally neutral. Its use in actual life-situations determines whether it is good or bad. This means that not all sex outside of marriage is bad, and conversely (and somewhat frighteningly for those of us who are married) that not all sex within marriage is good. Christian teaching has oscillated from teaching that sex is evil and thus to be avoided, to teaching that it is very good and thus to be reserved for marriage. In the Age of the Pill we can assert that sex is neutral.

For too long we have allowed sex to rule our lives —an inheritance perhaps from ancient pagan religions and the mystery that surrounded man's inability to control sex. We have been slaves to sex, to our fears of conception, to the taboos we have established in this realm. In the Age of the Pill this situation can change; it *must* change.

Consider as an illustration of the tyranny of sexuality its domination of our language. How is it, for example, that the word "fidelity" has come to be understood primarily as relating to sexual behavior? Is there no way a woman can be unfaithful to her husband other than by going to bed with another man? We have similarly allowed sex to dominate our understanding of such words as "chastity," "nice girl," "good boy," "obscene," "prostitute," "lover," "pregnant." And all these words have alternate meanings which are totally nonsexual. Why have we tolerated the tyranny of sex? Sex should be our servant, not our master. And we live with the certitude of that fact in the Age of the Pill.

The power of sex to control thoughts and lives is well illustrated by the comments of a bright and well adjusted college sophomore with whom I have discussed these matters. He put it this way: "Sex is the ultimate, the very essence of human existence. As such it should be reserved for marriage. It should be learned by a man and his wife in the love relationship. Virginity until marriage is the only way that the significance of sex can be protected." Now I admire this young man for his stand. Few young people have the courage to admit to a group of their peers that they are virgins at age 20. And I shall defend my friend's right to remain a virgin despite the pressures of his environment. *But*—what happens if he is seduced? Will he feel obligated to marry a girl he does not love? What if he falls in love with a girl only to learn that she is sexually experienced? Will this make marriage to a girl he loves an impossibility?

To be sure, there are perils in living with a demythologized sexuality. But there are also great perils inherent in our traditional understanding of sex. Perhaps my young friend would have a better chance of living successfully with sex—even with his commitment to preserving his own virginity—had he not placed sex on so high a pedestal.

A college coed being interviewed for a TV documentary summed it up well: "It's not so important any more *whether* you are or are not a virgin. What counts is *why* you are or are not a virgin."

Nonmarital sex, then, can be good. It appears that it already is good for some people, and it can be good for others if the church will bring the gospel to bear on post-Pill sexuality. Guilt about sex may have had value when it prevented an involvement that might have ruined several lives by producing an unwanted child; but in the Age of the Pill such guilt is anachronistic. With a more enlightened outlook the church could stop encouraging marriages based on sexual desire alone. It could reduce the number of young men who choose depersonalized sex with a prostitute rather than loving sex with their fiancées out of concern for the latter's "purity." These and many other abuses encouraged by the church's current attitudes toward sex could be reduced if the church would make relevant application of the gospel to contemporary sexuality. (Some ministers, of course, are already giving meaningful help to their parishioners in these matters—often risking their positions and reputations. Their courage is to be applauded; their minority status must be deplored.)

In this quest for a relevant Christian sex ethic we must be guided by the Bible but not oppressed by its "thou shalt nots." Unconditional biblical prohibitions, along with 99 per cent of the Christian writing which has attempted to interpret them, are out of date, are part of the Pre-Pill Age. A relevant ethic cannot be appropriated *in toto* from another time. It has fallen to this generation to be the first to live in the Age of the Pill. We must find specific answers to the challenges it brings.

Like the prohibition against eating pork (a meat which in those days was almost always worm-ridden), the Old Testament prohibition against nonmarital intercourse was a good rule for its time—especially in light of the importance that Jewish society placed on a pure bloodline. And in the time of Jesus and throughout the nearly two milleniums of the church's life the teaching that sex should be reserved for marriage was sound, since the begetting of children outside of marriage was (and is) socially undesirable. But such a sweeping rule is no longer needed. Avoidance of nonmarital sex will not *always* be best for *all* people— indeed, the very opposite can be and sometimes is the case.

For some time now theologians of "liberal bent"

have been hinting at the emergence of a "new morality." They have been brave enough to say that nonmarital sex is not necessarily wrong. Now we must go further and proclaim that, properly understood and lovingly practiced, sex outside of marriage is indeed a positive good. The Pill and the scientific discoveries that will follow it mean that for the first time nonmarital sex can be a loving interpersonal relationship.

But—lest the would-be hedonists begin their rejoicing too quickly—there is more to be said. Much more. The old morality cannot immediately be swept away; it is too powerful for that. The changes chronicled above and the call for an ethic that is truly contemporary do not mean that man has been freed for sanctified hedonism. This new age of less-inhibited sexuality requires of man a new kind of responsibility, of the church a new kind of leadership. It was relatively easy to be "moral" under the hard and fast rules of pre-Pill Christianity. It will be more difficult to deal with the possibilities wrought by the advent of oral contraception.

We are moving into a transitional period which will be difficult for the law, for the church and for the individual member of the society—especially for the man who seeks to be true to the gospel. In this awkward time we shall be living with the reality of the new morality and with the very real and powerful residue of the old. It would be totally unrealistic to believe that because we have intellectually done away with the old prohibitions they have no power. They will continue to influence the society which judges individual actions. And, like it or not, even those who feel they have completely swept the old morality from their minds are troubled at one time or another as a consequence of its haunting effect. Even Hugh Hefner and his feminine counterpart Helen Gurley Brown occasionally show signs of the influence of the old code morality.

We cannot ignore the stigmas that our society as a whole (at least on the surface, for show) stamps on offenders under the old rules. And since these marks of disapproval are very much a part of the lives of the young people whom churchmen must counsel, we cannot ignore them. We must teach our young people that these rules are still powerful social forces which cannot be cavalierly ignored.

Meanwhile the church should be seeking to weaken rather than strengthen the hold of pre-Pill morality on society. Creative guidance demands that the church be an agent for re-education rather than a defender of the status quo.

But the responsibilities of the church do not end with recognition of and opposition to the old codes. It must protect the personal integrity of all people. It must proclaim loudly that the right to say No to the new morality is inalienable. It must defend those who in good conscience wish to remain loyal to the traditional code. Our sexually liberated society needs the church to help it avoid overreacting and falling on its face as the bonds which have restrained it are cut. To put it another way: the church must help prevent sexual freedom from becoming sexual idolatry.

Perhaps of greatest importance is the church's task of helping man guard himself against rationalization and the misuse of his new freedom. We do not yet know if man is able to handle the freedom the Pill brings. Some will insist that he is not. (And the history of man's use of the airplane, nuclear fission and the like would seem to bear out the contentions of such pessimists.) But if—and this is a very large IF—man can respond responsibly to this new situation, then loving, nondestructive, nonsinful, recreational sex is a possibility in the Age of the Pill.

True, the temptations of this new epoch will be myriad. The sexually liberated Christian man will be tempted to take advantage of girls who have not yet worked out their own personal ethics. That is to say, the argument in favor of sexual freedom can be used as a "line" by one bent on seduction. One who embraces the new morality will be tempted to substitute a shallow sexual relationship for a more meaningful, well rounded one. He will be tempted to ignore the feelings of others, to become overly concerned with surface values, to insult those whose views on sex are different from his. In short, we will be tempted to misuse demythologized sex in all the ways we are currently tempted to misuse beer, cards, leisure time, celluloid film and all the rest of the processes and artifacts that surround us. In the face of this challenge, the church is called to witness.

Preservation of the family or some similar structure in which children can be reared into responsible adulthood will be a top priority of society and the church as we begin to live with the new morality. Other problems will arise and demand our attention. And the time to begin working toward their solution is NOW.

The church must begin at once to take whatever steps are feasible in a given locale. To be sure, intensive biblical and theological studies are needed, but we cannot allow their state of incompletion to be an excuse for silence. The church must begin now with sex education for children, youth and adults. Our teaching of ethics must emphasize loving responses to the challenges of real situations and not the automatic application of some time-worn rule to all similar challenges. In our counseling we churchmen must be realistic enough to admit the existence of and deal with premarital sex among "nice boys and girls," the pressures of single adulthood and the unwanted feelings of guilt which incapacitate many young married persons. These very real problems cannot be ignored. We can further strive for a new toleration of and love for those who trespass the old morality. We can begin to make distinctions between the various kinds of nonmarital sex so that at least our expressions of disapproval may become quantitatively appropriate. We must do away with that mind-set which infers that loving sex with one's fiancée and the rape of a 12-year-old are equal crimes deserving equal condemnation.

The challenges are many—and exceedingly complex. But unless the church acts decisively with some positive steps toward a creative and relevant sex ethic, it is doomed to be ignored.

THE OLD IMMORALITY

BY BILLY GRAHAM

Some time ago a friend and I were walking down Oxford Street in London, when we saw what appeared to be an actress or model getting into a chauffeured limousine while a small crowd gathered to watch. Several photographers begged her to get out of the car so that they could get better pictures. When she complied, they began to yell: "Pull your dress down at the top. The editors won't use the pictures unless you do."

Today every area of our lives is invaded by this immoral flare, which leaves no one untouched. In many of our publications and in most of our entertainment, the emphasis is on sex appeal. Even churchmen, having failed to locate the cause or to produce a remedy for this disease of man, now talk about a "new morality" to fit the times; but their so-called new morality is nothing more than the old immorality brought up to date.

Evidence of the moral disintegration of our society appears everywhere we look. A senator told me recently: "Every time we appoint an investigating committee to investigate anything, it turns up snakes!" It seems that we have gone back to the days of Noah and come full cycle to what Jesus prophesied would take place when he said: "But as the days of Noah were, so shall also the coming of the Son of man be" (Matt. 24:37). He reaffirmed the Old Testament account of a social and moral disintegration so bad that God allowed the world to be destroyed by a flood in the days of Noah. He said also that moral history would repeat itself and that this same moral disintegration would be characteristic of the era just preceding the end of history as we know it.

The concern for Western man's moral dissolution is not confined to sociologists, psychologists, preachers, and professors. It is the concern of political leaders, military leaders, business and professional people, and trade union leaders. It is the concern of newspaper editors such as Jenkins Lloyd Jones of the Tulsa *Tribune*, who declared in an address to a convention of newspaper editors that our people have decided that sin is largely imaginary. We have become enamored of a psychology that holds that man is a product of his heredity and a victim of his environment. Mr. Jones said: "We have sown the dragon's teeth of pseudoscientific sentimentality, and out of the ground has sprung the legion bearing switchblade knives and bicycle chains. Clearly something is missing."

Taking a look at Hollywood, editor Jones said: "Can anyone deny that movies are dirtier than ever? But they don't call it dirt. They call it 'realism.' Why do we let them fool us? Why do we nod owlishly when they tell us that filth is merely a daring art form, that licentiousness is really social comment?"

In the face of this legalized pornography, the conscience of America seems to be paralyzed. More serious than our fakery in art, literature, and pictures is the collapse of our moral standards and the blunting of our capacity as a nation for righteous indignation. We seem to be insensible to the rowdiness of the stage, the glorification of burlesque, the drowning of our youngsters in the violence, cynicism, and sadism that is piped into the living room and even the nursery via television. We are struck dumb in the presence of bawdy-house literature, which fills our best-seller lists with risqué novels that belong in the brothel. One newspaper executive had the courage to ask his book department to quit advertising morally objectionable literature in the list of best sellers. We are accused of tampering with the facts. But what facts? There are the facts of immorality, degeneracy, and whoremongering. These are not only American facts. They are facts that should put a blush on the flags of almost every nation under the sun.

It has always been a mark of decaying civilization to become obsessed with sex. When people lose their way, their purpose, their will, and their goals, as well as their faith, like the ancient Israelites, they go "a whoring." It is a form of diversion that requires no thought, no character, and no restraint. One of the world's great historians told me: "The moral deterioration in the West will destroy us by the year 2000 A.D. even if the Communists don't!"

Pornography

Our Western society has become so obsessed with sex that it seeps from all the pores of our national life. Formerly, novelists wove the subject subtly into their stories as a part of life. But today from the pens of D. H. Lawrence, Norman Mailer, Henry Miller, and a hundred lesser lights pours a stream of perverse, vulgar, and even obscene writings like the drippings from a broken sewer. Sex is front page copy everywhere.

The question is, does freedom of speech and the

202 ·   SEX

press imply the freedom to corrupt the minds of the
people through mass media, thus inciting every form of
sexual perversion and immorality? We have laws in our
cities forbidding open sewers and cesspools. Why
shouldn't we have laws forbidding pornography and
obscenity? Many heroic leaders have tried, but they
have stumbled over even the definition of the word
"obscenity." If we cannot agree on the length of a foot,
it is because we have lost our yardstick. No one has
ever improved upon the moral yardstick given to man
in the Ten Commandments. Pornography is anything
that depicts lewdness in such a way as to create impure
thoughts and lusts. However, the sewers continue to
flow, destroying the moral fabric of our society, until
they have become the greatest threat to our security.

So-called artistic realism, which is both the goal
and guiding star of some parts of the motion picture industry in Europe and America, adds up to filth, rotten-
ness, dirt, and animated pornography that is feeding
our youth with poison. No wonder young people are
sexually sophisticated at sixteen.

We are corrupting the imagination and taste of a
whole generation. Love is perverted to Sodom lust.
Sensibilities are so hardened that domestic crimes and
international atrocities are accepted as matters of
course.

No one can doubt that dirty appetites are becoming the principal satisfaction of life. In this way we
are permitting the diabolic to triumph. Jeremiah the
prophet warned: "Were they ashamed when they had
committed abomination? nay, they were not at all
ashamed, neither could they blush; therefore they shall
fall among them that fall: at the time that I visit them
they shall be cast down, saith the Lord" (Jer. 6:15).

Dr. P. A. Sorokin, one of the most astute observers of America's sex scene and former professor of
sociology at Harvard University, says: "There has been

a growing preoccupation of our writers with the social sewers, the broken homes of disloyal parents and unloved children, the bedroom of the prostitute, a cannery row brothel, a den of criminals, a ward of the insane, a club of dishonest politicians, a street corner gang of teen-age delinquents, a hate-laden prison, a crime-ridden waterfront, the courtroom of a dishonest judge, the sex adventures of urbanized cavemen and rapists, the loves of adulterers and fornicators, of masochists, sadists, prostitutes, mistresses, playboys. Juicy loves, id, orgasms, and libidos are seductively prepared and served with all the trimmings.''

Ancient historians tell us that one of the symptoms of a declining civilization is a desexualization of the human race, with men becoming more effeminate and women becoming more masculine, not only in physical characteristics but in their basic characters.

Perversion

Hand in hand with this desexualization appears the sinister form of perversion so increasingly evident in our society today, of such a nature that the old-fashioned sins look almost wholesome in contrast. Nothing can alter the fact that God calls perversion sin. ''There is therefore no possible defense for their conduct . . . God has given them up to shameful passions. Their women have exchanged natural intercourse for unnatural, and their men in turn, giving up natural relations with women, burn with lust for one another; males behave indecently with males, and are paid in their own persons the fitting wage of such perversion'' (Rom. 1:20–27, NEB).

The immutable law of sowing and reaping has held sway. We are now the hapless possessors of moral depravity, and we seek in vain for a cure. The tares of indulgence have overgrown the wheat of moral restraint. Our homes have suffered. Divorce has grown to epidemic proportions. When the morals of society are upset, the family is the first to suffer. The home is the basic unit of our society, and a nation is only as strong as her homes. The breaking up of a home does not often make headlines, but it eats like termites at the structure of the nation.

As a result of the mounting divorces, separations, and desertions, about twelve million of the forty-five million children in the United States do not live with both parents. A vicious circle is set in motion. As the Bible says: "The fathers have eaten a sour grape, and the children's teeth are set on edge" (Jer. 31:29).

In every area of our social life we see operating the inevitable law of diminishing returns in our obsession with sex. Many do something for a thrill only to find the next time that they must increase the dose to produce the same thrill. As the kick wears off, they are driven to look for new means, for different experiences to produce a comparable kick. The sex glutton is tormented by feelings of guilt and remorse. His mode of living is saturated with intense strain, unnatural emotions, and inner conflicts. His personality is thwarted in its search for development. His passions are out of control, and the end result is frustration. In his defiance of God's law and society's norm, he puts a death-dealing tension on his soul. His search for new thrills, for new kicks, for exciting experiences keeps him in the grip of fear, insecurity, doubt, and futility. Dr. Sorokin says: "The weakened physical, emotional, and spiritual condition of the sex glutton usually makes him incapable of resisting the accompanying pressures, and he eventually cracks under their weight. He often ends by becoming a psychoneurotic or a suicide."

The warning of the Bible is clear. In Hebrews 13:4 the scripture says: "Whoremongers and adulterers God will judge." Those who scoff at the idea of judgment would do well to study the latest statistics on illegitimate births and venereal diseases. Illegitimate births are at an all-time high; venereal disease rages at epidemic proportions throughout the nation; and all this in the face of the latest in contraceptives and antibiotics. The Scripture says: "Be not deceived: neither fornicators, nor idolators, nor adulterers, nor effeminate, nor abusers of themselves with mankind . . . shall inherit the kingdom of God" (I Cor. 6:9).

One of the most disturbing features of the situation is the attitude of certain Protestant clergymen. *Time* magazine says: "Protestant churchmen are beginning to change their attitude. They are no longer shaking their finger because boys and girls give in to natural biological urges and experiment. They don't say 'Stop, you are wrong!' but 'Is it meaningful?' " Many pastors and university chaplains now openly condone premarital sex.

Ours is an age of moral relativism. However, there are certain areas in which the Scriptures do not allow us to negotiate. In all of these centuries there has not been the slightest shadow of change in the nature of God or in His attitude toward sin. The Bible teaches from beginning to end that adultery and fornication are sin, and the attitude of certain modern churchmen does not alter its character.

Dishonesty

But we must not leave the impression that sexual immorality is the only sphere of moral danger in our civilization. Dishonesty has increased in our society to alarming proportions. I sat in a federal court to hear the case of a highly respected member of the medical profession who had willfully and deliberately falsified his income tax. He was sentenced to ten years in a federal prison.

The disease of dishonesty invades every profession, and its spread into our society is alarming even to the most apathetic among us. The sports scandals shocked the nation as young amateur athletes sold out their ideals and ethics to the hoodlums and gangsters. It has been known for years that professional boxing is deeply infiltrated by the rackets, and the investigations which revealed that the throwing of fights is common practice came as no surprise to many. In a recent survey on a college campus, it was found that seventy-five percent of the students admitted to cheating sometime during their college careers.

Recently as I rode from the airport of a major city in a taxi, I engaged in conversation with the taxi driver. He said: "Payoffs are the practice at every level in the city. If the business house does not pay off, they will just dig up the street in front of the house and keep it that way for a year. When I get my cab inspected, I have to pay twenty-five dollars under the table. The man who collects says he only gets to keep five." He said: "If you took the payoff out of the city, the economy of the city would collapse."

John Steinbeck wrote a letter to Adlai Stevenson in which he said: "There is a creeping all-pervading gas of immorality which starts in the nursery and does not stop until it reaches the highest offices both corporate and governmental." Walter Lippmann says: "America is beginning to accept a new code of ethics that allows for chiseling and lying."

Why is there all this dishonesty in every phase of our life? Russell Kirk tells us why: "All this century, this columnist suspects, honesty in great things and small has been diminishing in most of the world. Public and private honesty is produced in part by religious convictions . . . when religious sanctions decay . . . the average sensual man tends to cheat."

A dying culture

That moral and spiritual decadence is upon us today becomes evident at the turn of every page of our daily newspaper. We live in a day when old values are rejected and the sense of significance and purpose has disappeared from many people's lives. The Western world's sole objective seems to be success, status, security, self-indulgence, pleasure, and comfort. If we can judge our times by the paintings produced by some modern artists, we see indiscriminate splashes of color with no recognizable pattern or design. A child throwing paint on the canvas could do as well. As a matter of fact, at one art exhibit a chimpanzee won first prize for his painting. The incomprehensible mixture of pigment merely denotes the confused minds and values of our day. The playwright, the novelist, and the movie scriptwriter all give us unadulterated doses of violence, sex, and murder. This would indeed seem to be a sick generation in need of salvation. The cause of our trouble was revealed recently in a statement by Tennessee Williams, one of the most widely read playwrights of our day, when he said: "We have very little conviction of our own essential dignity, or even of our essential decency" (*Missions*, January 1962).

With all this evidence of decadence in view it is no wonder that May Craig, Washington correspondent, says: "Unless there is a change deep down in the American people, a genuine crusade against self-indulgence and immorality, public and private, then we are witnesses to the decline and fall of the American Republic."

Yes, we need to cry out to be saved—saved from ourselves, for it is the soul of a nation and a culture that is dying! Hosea the prophet urged the people of his day: "Sow to yourselves in righteousness, reap in mercy; break up your fallow ground: for it is time to seek the Lord, till he come and rain righteousness upon you'' (Hos. 10:12).

The crack in the moral dam is widening, but like the people of Noah's day before the flood, life goes on as usual with only a few concerned and scarcely anyone alarmed. However, apathy will not deter catastrophe. The people of Noah's day were not expecting judgment—but it came! We have become soft and comfortable. Watching television, I notice that when almost any crisis arises on the screen, the actor usually says: ''Give me a drink.'' When the headlines get black and foreboding, the sale of alcohol and barbiturates rises in the country, as millions try to escape from the grim realities of our dangers.

In a seminar on a university campus a student asked me: ''Is our society in the process of dying, or is it committing the hypocrisy of being dead without knowing it?'' I answered: ''I am not sure; but I am alarmed, and I feel the burden and compulsion of the prophets of old to warn the people. Whether they listen or not is really not my responsibility.'' Time after time the prophets warned the people of old, but the Scriptures say that their hearts became hardened and their ears deaf. They were deliberately deaf to the Word of God.

This we do know, our decaying morals do not surprise God. They add to the pile of inflammable tinder that shall someday be ignited by the fires of God's judgment. The words of the Apostle Paul in the first chapter of Romans, addressed to the decadent Roman society, might well apply to us: ''Because that, when they knew God, they glorified Him not as God, neither were thankful'' (Rom. 1:21). If ever a generation was bequeathed the knowledge of God, we were. Yet we are throwing away this glorious heritage on our lust and passions.

Again Paul said: "But became vain in their imaginations, and their foolish heart was darkened. Professing themselves to be wise, they became fools" (Rom. 1:21, 22). The word "became" suggests deterioration and decay. In a decadent society, the will to believe, to resist, to contend, to fight, to struggle is gone. In place of this will to resist, there is the desire to conform, to drift, to follow, to yield, and to give up. This is what happened to Rome, but it applies to us. The same conditions that prevailed in Rome prevail in our society. Before Rome fell, her standards were abandoned, the family disintegrated, divorce prevailed, immorality was rampant, and faith was at a low ebb. As Gibbon said: "There was much talk of religion but few practiced it." Today our churches are filled, but how many are actually practicing Christianity in daily life?

Again Paul said: "(They) changed the glory of the incorruptible God into an image made like to corruptible man" (Rom. 1:23). Humanism has become the God of our time. Aldous Huxley spoke of "human control by human effort in accordance with human ideals." The modern creed of "I believe in man" is a complete reversal of Biblical theology.

The great Apostle again said: "Wherefore God also gave them up to uncleanness, through the lusts of their own hearts, to dishonor their own bodies between themselves" (Rom. 1:24). It does not say that God gave up, only that God gave man up to unclean and unrighteous practices. When this happens, we are in terrifying danger!

Thus three times in this passage from Romans it tells that God gave man up. In one instance, God gave them up when man turned to immoral lust and practices. In another instance, God gave them up when man turned to vile affections and to immoral deviations. In yet another instance, God gave them up when man turned to a reprobate mind and became filled with all unrighteousness, fornication, covetousness, and maliciousness.

When God gives man up, there is only one thing left—judgment! Here it is: "Who, knowing the judgment of God, that they which commit such things are worthy of death, not only do the same, but have pleasure in them that do them" (Rom. 1:32). When Sodom and Gomorrah became guilty of the same sins that we commit, God judged them with fire and brimstone. The Bible says: "God spared them not." When the people of Noah's day became guilty of these same sins, the Bible says: "God spared them not."

We cannot claim to be God's pets. We have no special dispensation from judgment. If we continue on our present course, the moral law that says "the wages of sin is death" (Rom. 6:23) will mean ultimate death to our society.

How ironic it is that a civilization that has produced the best automobiles, the best refrigerators, and the best television sets is at the same time producing some of the worst human beings. The total answer to our dilemma in this debacle is that we have forsaken God. God's indictment of man is summed up in four words: "They are without excuse" (Rom. 1:20). We as a nation are without excuse, because we have bartered our birthright for a mess of immoral delights. We are finding out that what de Tocqueville said is true: "When America ceases to be good, it will cease to be great."

In our knowledge, which has become foolishness, we are setting the stage for personal and national dissolution and ultimate judgment. We are heaping high for conflagration. We are building for destruction. We are begging for judgment. Thomas Jefferson said: "I tremble for my country when I remember God is just." "Verily I say unto you, it shall be more tolerable for the land of Sodom and Gomorrah in the day of judgment," said Jesus (Matt. 10:15).

In the King Tut museum in Cairo there is a grain of wheat five thousand years old taken from the tombs of the Pharaohs. It is said that if the seed were planted, it would grow. The seeds of integrity, reverence, and righteousness are not dead; but we are not allowing them to germinate. There is still time The day is far spent, it is true; but it is not too late for us to stay the catastrophic fires of God's judgment. The Bible declares: "(God is) not willing that any should perish" (II Pet. 3:9). And again the Bible declares: "To-day if ye will hear his voice, harden not your hearts" (Heb. 3:7, 8).

A CHRISTIAN VIEW OF CONTRACEPTION

BY M. O. VINCENT

From the Bible the Christian derives moral principles that he deductively applies to specific situations. Ethical decisions are motivated by love for God and our fellow men, guided by the Holy Spirit and reason. Although there is no specific text in Scripture to settle the contraception issue, the overall scriptural view of the nature of God, man, marriage, and sexual intercourse leads to the conclusion that we have a right to control conception.

God, the Creator and Sustainer of mankind, created us male and female. He designed us physically so that sex relations were possible. And he designed us emotionally with desire that makes sex relations prob-

Merville O. Vincent is assistant medical superintendent of Homewood Sanitarium, Guelph, Ontario. He holds the B.A. from Acadia University and the M.D. and C.M. from Dalhousie University. Dr. Vincent is a fellow in psychiatry of the Royal College of Physicians (Canada).

"A Christian View of Contraception" appeared in the book Birth Control and the Christian *(Tyndale House Publishers, Wheaton, Illinois) and is reprinted here by permission.*

able. God saw that each thing he created was good;
sex is of God, and therefore sex is good.

God created man with reason, judgment, a sense
of responsibility, and a will. Therefore man is not governed just by instinct. He can direct many affairs in his
own life; he has freedom to use God's gifts according
to his own condition and circumstances. God gave man
dominion over the earth, and when man the creature
fell, God even gave his Son to be man and to redeem
man. The reconciled man therefore seeks God's will,
so that he may exercise his dominion responsibly, for
God made man responsible to him. To subdue and
have dominion over nature in a manner demonstrating
love both to God and to our fellow men is a Christian
principle apparent throughout Scripture, from the first
chapter of Genesis.

"And God blessed them, and God said to them, be
fruitful and multiply. . . ." Here we note that "be fruitful and multiply" was given by God more as a blessing
than a commandment, and certainly not as a curse. If
the human race ceased to be fruitful and multiply, it
would disappear in one generation. But God did not
say whether we were to multiply by one, two, or ten.

Marriage is an institution ordained by God, and
Scripture shows that it has several functions:

1. We do not read in Scripture that woman was
created primarily for the propagation of the species;
rather, she was created because it was "not good that
the man should be alone." God's plan provided for a
companion who would satisfy the unfulfilled yearning
of man's heart. Woman was created for mutual fellowship and companionship with man, as one with whom
he would share love, trust, devotion, and responsibility. This loving companionship, if not the prime scriptural purpose of marriage, is at least as important as
the procreative function.

2. Obviously marriage has a procreative function,

related, by God's design, to intercourse. But nowhere
does Scripture restrict sex relations to the sole purpose
of procreation.

3. In fact, one function of the sexual relationship
in marriage that Paul mentions might be called that of
a "moral prophylaxis" (I Cor. 7:9); that is, marriage
prevents sexual irregularities in society.

Sexual intercourse is intimately involved with the
two major purposes of marriage, companionship and
procreation. Its relation to procreation is obvious. However, it also has an important unitive function. While
biologically it decreases tension, it involves much more
than biology. It involves all the personality, and at its
highest level it is a medium of deep communication—
physically, psychologically, and spiritually—of concepts
and feelings that defy verbal expression: of love, commitment of the whole life, security, interdependence.
Oscar E. Feucht has said:

> God made marriage for sex and sex for marriage.
> God made sex one of the means for continuously
> uniting a man and his wife in the deepest and
> most realistic way, a unique way in which they
> are "known" to each other as they could not
> otherwise know each other, in the fullest expres-
> sion of mutual love unlike any other demonstra-
> tion. The "one flesh" concept is basic and
> dominant in the Bible's teaching on marriage
> (Gen. 2:24; Exod. 21:10; Lev. 18; Deut. 24:5;
> Matt. 19:5, 6; Mark 10:6–8; I Cor. 7:2–6; Eph.
> 5:31) [*Sex and the Church*, p. 218].

Three additional points call for mention:
1. The scriptural sequence is that marriage pre-
cedes intercourse. Therefore fornication, adultery, and
prostitution, with or without contraceptives, are not a
Christian option.
2. Sharing and meeting each other's sexual needs

is so important that Paul advises against prolonged
abstinence (I Cor. 7: 3–5) and implies frequent sexual
relations as the norm in marriage, without any mention
of procreation.

3. Nowhere does Scripture say that intercourse
may not be engaged in primarily for mutual pleasure
and satisfaction. God established a physical attraction
between the sexes. In the marriage relationship, as the
Song of Solomon stresses, sex is a sensuous delight that
is to have its normal, healthy role in providing fulfillment and joy for both partners. It is not to be shunned
but to be praised.

If, then, Scripture teaches that sexual union has
functions other than procreation, under certain conditions conception may be hindered while the other
functions are filled. I believe the case is clear that the
Christian has a right to control conception.

Most families have some need for contraception,
both for their own well-being and for the well-being of
society. Whenever a child would be a significant emotional, physical, or economic burden to either a wife
or a husband, the couple should consider before God
the advisability of having such a child, whether it would
be the tenth or the first.

Contraception is the means of preventing the
birth of unwanted children. Nothing is more detrimental to a child than to feel that his parents wish he
had not been born. Scripture emphasizes the concept of
responsible parenthood (I Tim. 5:8). It is irresponsible
for a couple to bring more children into the world than
they can nurture spiritually, financially, emotionally,
and educationally.

Society as a whole is confronted by the population
explosion. In treating disease, we physicians have
taken seriously God's command to subdue nature and
have drastically decreased the death rate. The result is
a population that is outstripping food supply and eco-

nomic development. World population was under two billion in 1920 but by 1960 was almost three billion. If the present rate of growth continues, it will be seven and one-half billion by the end of the century. Faced with this acute problem, should we not make as great an effort to prevent new life as to prolong existing life? I believe the Christian's concern for his neighbor requires him not only to think seriously about the size of his own family but also to become involved in worldwide educational plans that seek to help people see the wisdom of limiting family size.

No person or no law can tell a couple how many children they should have or how they should be spaced. This decision is in the area of Christian liberty. Christians know their entire lives—including their sex lives—belong to God; therefore, they must act with love rather than selfishness. They must observe the times and circumstances in which they are living and, through reason and the guidance of the Holy Spirit, seek to make responsible decisions.

Some factors to be weighed are:

1. Can all the needs of the children—physical, emotional, spiritual, economic, and educational—be met if another child is added?

2. Will another child affect the emotional or physical well-being of the mother or father?

3. Over-production of children may be as sinful as selfish avoidance of parenthood.

4. Economic reasons for contraception are not necessarily selfish. "But if any provide not for his own, and especially for those of his own house, he hath denied the faith, and is worse than an infidel" (I Tim. 5:8).

5. What is the likelihood of genetically transmitted illness?

6. Some couples do not like children and would

method. It too is frequently ineffective. And it interferes with the naturalness and spontaneity of the sexual act by ruling out sex relations around the time of ovulation, when sexual desire in the female is often increased.

Sterilization is a method of contraception, and so the moral principles that apply to other methods of contraception apply to sterilization as well. The significant difference is that it is permanent. When a couple feel convinced that they must not have any more children, they might reasonably decide that one of them should be sterilized.

Contraception in Christian marriage not only is permissible but has a very significant value. This point should be made firmly, clearly, and loudly, for the benefit of all Christians who may have lingering doubts.

make poor parents. I believe they have a right to ma
tal companionship without children.

If the motive for contraception is proper, is
method used of ethical significance? I heartily con
with the statement made by the Augustana Synod
the Lutheran Church:

> The means which a married pair uses to determ
> the number and the spacing of the births of t
> children are a matter for them to decide with t
> own consciences, on the basis of competent r
> ical advice and in a sense of accountability
> God. So long as it causes no harm to those
> volved either immediately or over an exter
> period, none of the methods for controlling
> number and spacing of the births of childrer
> any special moral merit or demerit. It is the
> in which the means is used, rather than whetl
> is "natural or artificial," which defines its "
> ness" or "wrongness." "Whatever you do,
> to the glory of God" (I Cor. 10:31) is a pri
> pertinent to the use of the God-given reprod
> power.

To deal with specific methods, then, lies outsi
purpose of this paper. But I would like to co
briefly on three methods. Abstinence is undou
the most effective means of contraception. Howe
defeats the whole purpose of sexual intercourse i
riage. Unless it is completely satisfactory to bo
band and wife, it would be considered immo
cording to the seventh chapter of First Corinthia

Coitus interruptus (withdrawal prior to
tion) is generally unsatisfactory. It often is
logically frustrating for husband and wife, a
unreliable.

There are two major objections to the

JEWISH COLLEGE PRESIDENT OPPOSES CONTRACEPTION

BY EFFIE ALLEY

While many Catholic theologians, scholars and laity indict the Pope's ban against artificial contraception as an attempt to turn the clock back, a Jewish professor of law and social science welcomes it as showing what time of day it really is.

Dr. Victor G. Rosenblum, who left Northwestern University recently to become president of Reed College in Portland, Oregon, believes the Pope may turn out to have been more farsighted than his critics.

Terming the much debated encyclical a "document of confrontation" for modern society, he said:

"It is something for all of us to confront in determining what the acceptable policy in a democratic society ought to be."

As founder and director of Northwestern's program in law and social sciences, Rosenblum is keenly interested in the attitudes of society, the things that engender them and the policies into which they eventually harden.

He sees the current widespread preoccupation with contraception as a possible threat to social evolu-

Effie Alley is science writer for Chicago Today.

tion along truly human and humanitarian lines because, in his phrase, "it tends to warp some of the most significant of our human traits—compassion and love."

He continued:

"Our preoccupation with birth limitation contains the seeds of some very troublesome attitudes, indifference or callousness to the needs of others and a very crass form of materialism."

These are to be seen even now wherever you look, the professor maintains.

In private life, in the growing number of couples who say they would like to have a child but can't afford it, thus equating the value of a child with material goods. Among mothers who before they send their girls off to college see to it that they have an adequate supply of The Pill—just in case.

"This is the most horrible form of indifference," Prof. Rosenblum said, "because it says as plainly as possible 'our concern is not with you but only that you don't cause us trouble, and meanwhile we'll do all we can to make you totally irresponsible by seeing to it that never in your life will you have to make a decision which counts.'"

The same thing is reflected in our attitude toward social problems, those of the inner city, for instance.

"If we believe these problems can be solved by cutting down the birth of children," said Rosenblum, "we are modern Malthusians, not the humanitarians we think we are.

"Because the families of the black poor are larger than ours, we feel we must teach them contraceptive practices so they can conform to our standards.

"If they don't we blame them for creating their own misery and say it is all of their own fault.

"If nothing else, the Pope's pronouncement is supportive of the poor man who has a large family right now." It says to him, "We know your difficulties and we don't think you should have to face them alone. Everyone must be concerned to see that your children are fed, educated, given their chance in life.

"Had the encyclical gone the other way, it would have put a social onus on people with large families."

Rosenblum has no bone to pick with people who want free choice of family size. What concerns him is that it continues to be free. And he very much doubts that it will if we see no impediment to use of contraception and other forms of birth limitation condemned by the Pope—abortion and sterilization—as tools for human and social engineering.

Coercion of this kind may be nearer than most people think.

Population experts have already questioned more than once whether couples—particularly those considered by geneticists as poor breeding stock—have the right to determine the number of children they will have.

Fertility researchers in a score of laboratories are right now looking for what they believe would be the ideal contraceptive—something that could be implanted at adolescence to make women permanently infertile, unless it is removed.

This would truly make every child a wanted child.

The question in Rosenblum's mind is, wanted by whom? The parents or the state? For the illiterate, the disadvantaged, the genetically dubious, the ideologically suspect, the baby quota might always be full.

Meanwhile there are social and economic pressures that can be exercised toward the same goal.

Even today the federal government has a heavy investment in contraceptive projects, designed particularly for welfare clients.

Just recently, the department of health, education and welfare told authorities of two states—Massachusetts and Wisconsin—to make contraceptive help available to unmarried women or lose federal funds for aid to dependent children—and no matter about the state laws that prohibit the practice.

Also recent is the proposal of a New York legislator for a "baby tax" to be levied for all children of any couple in excess of two.

Commenting on these developments, Rosenblum said:

"There is always the tendency to convert a 'may' into a 'must'." We are now reaching the danger point where the welfare bureaucracy is impelled to make permitted birth control mandatory.

"From this point, it may be a shorter step than we realize to the naming of expert committees to decide who shall be born, when and with what traits."

And if man, acting for the state, can say who should be born, may he not also claim the right to say who shall live and for how long? Since the aged are also often a liability along with the deformed, the retarded, the social misfits and the insane, could not these too be disposed of in the interest of a better life for the highly intelligent, well-motivated, carefully-selected few?

No reason at all why not if man comes to regard himself as "a natural creature like any other," as Dr. Robert L. Sinsheimer of California Institute of Technology says he must be taught to do if biological science is to achieve its full potential.

In Rosenblum's view the acceptance of contraception as an instrument of national policy could do a great deal to pave the way for human acceptance of education for dehumanization.

It is in its basic opposition to this trend that the Pope's encyclical has its significance for society as a whole, Rosenblum said.

"The Church's message may turn out to have been the means of keeping an organization such as the state from getting this type of control."

"While in general the state's position is for human and ideological conformity to whatever the prevailing ideas happen to be, the Church speaks for the whole range and richness of human diversity."

And this is the way Rosenblum thinks it ought to be. For it is in these human resources that he believes we will find the real solutions to the problems that confront us. He said:

"Why shouldn't we be able to develop new programs that will enable us to draw on our vast resources in human abilities, wherever they are?

"As an educator I couldn't think otherwise because I have learned that brilliance is where you find it. There is no formula by which it can be developed and it is not confined to any one class, group or race, but can be discovered throughout the range of human life. Our job is to search for it and nurture it.

Both as an educator and an individual, Rosenblum believes there are advantages in large families that more than compensated for the material deprivations they may have to sustain.

A member of a large family himself and the father of seven children ranging in age from 3 to 19, he says there is "a richness of life" in such a group scarcely obtainable elsewhere.

"I believe the home is a great place for education—especially the home with a number of children. Being involved with brothers and sisters, parents and relatives teaches love and affection, acceptance, tolerance, sharing and the proper handling of conflict—all good things for the individual and society."

Rosenblum laughs with the friends who send him Planned Parenthood literature on his wedding anniversaries but he is impatient with the people who sigh that they too would like a large family, if only they could afford it. Of them he says:

"Somehow there seems to be an idea that to have children you must first tote up your resources to make sure you can send them away to the best college, the best place, or just send them away."

"It may be that part of the revolt of youth today is a revolt against that kind of materialism. Maybe they are telling us that the real problems don't yield to a strictly economic solution."

"Perhaps they are indicating that they'd rather Dad would sit down and talk about their problems than furnish them with the latest car. In other words, that he'd allocate time instead of money."

"It's just possible that we might all have a better society if he did."

INHIBITIONS THROWN TO THE GENTLE WINDS

BY JANE HOWARD

A network of visionaries at work across America is convincing people by the thousands that human nature has been sold short. Collectively known as the Human Potential Movement, they include businessmen, psychologists, ex-weightlifters, professors, dancers and theologians. Though they disagree in many jargons on many points, they fervently concur that there is much more to life than most of us live, and that the world need not be as hypocritical, absurd and polluted as it is. It could change radically, they claim, if we'd let them guide us into real encounters with our own and each other's deepest, most vulnerable feelings.

The movement's methods, shown on the following pages, vary extravagantly. Some call for groups of people to recite dreams, confess secrets, don masks, go naked or gaze with unswerving honesty into each other's eyes for a full 10 minutes. The groups involved may celebrate their released feelings with an exuberant leap into the air.

Jane Howard is a staff writer for Life *magazine, and author of numerous human interest articles.*

"Inhibitions Thrown to the Gentle Winds" appeared in Life *magazine, July 12, 1968.* © *1968 Time, Inc.*

Some of these techniques provoke outrage and controversy, but all, based on a climate of trust and an ethic of relentless candor, are meant to draw us closer together faster than bomber crews in wartime—maybe than any people ever—and edge us toward a social utopia, and a feeling of joy, or, as the more messianic visionaries would have it, JOY!!

I began to get the spirit one morning with 11 other people at the movement's vortex, the Esalen Institute on the Big Sur coastline.

Anywhere else, even elsewhere on the map of the gloriously liberated state of California, people might have thought the 12 of us were crazy. We were supposed to be indoors starting another in our five-day series of encounter group meetings. We should have been interpersonally relating, interacting, honing and venting our feelings toward each other, and trading doses of a new commodity called feedback—the gift at last to see ourselves as others see us. ("You seem a *little* less uptight and eastern than you did yesterday" is a sample of the kind of feedback I kept getting.)

But we'd thrown our schedules, along with our inhibitions, to the gentle winds. Wildflowers bloomed on the mountainsides, flute music wafted from afar, and a whale was spouting in the ocean below. To go indoors on so dazzling a morning would have been obscene. Instead, before we knew it, we were making up individual, impromptu dances. "Let what wants to happen, happen!" cried Josie, the only real dancer among us. "Stay with the feeling! Make whatever noises you want to make, in time with your heartbeat! Flow!" Flow we did, or tried to. We swung, swooped, flailed and soared, shouting our rhythmic nonsense words. Mine sounded like a balloon caption from some paleolithic comic strip: "Froonga! FROONG-*GA*!"

We must have looked like the last scene of

Marat/Sade, but the people who saw us just smiled and went about their business, which like ours—and that of the 10,000 people who had preceded us to this marvelous Brigadoon of a place—was to be spontaneous. Crash courses in Spontaneity and Awareness, billed under dozens of headings and taught by experts both resident and itinerant, are Esalen's stock in trade. The courses usually cost $65 for a weekend seminar and $175 for a five-day workshop. The ever-changing student body, diverse as the raconteurs of the *Canterbury Tales*, includes ranchers, movie stars, associate professors, stockbrokers, priests, housewives, assistant buyers—all functioning, normal, certifiably "well" people.

But, in the view of Esalen's president and co-founder Michael Murphy, that isn't enough. "Normal" and "well" don't rule out anxiety, depression and alienation: "The idea is not emotional survival but emotional growth and improvement—not to adjust but to transcend. We don't try to make sick people well but well people better." Murphy, who graduated from Stanford University and spent 18 months studying meditation at an ashram in India long before such things became chic, thinks big. His goal, and Esalen's, and the movement's, is "the fulfillment of an ancient dream —reaching a terra incognita of consciousness." In 1962, when he inherited the 110-acre tract on which Esalen stands, he turned it into what his brochures now call "a center to explore those trends in the behavioral sciences, religion and philosophy which emphasize the potentialities and values of human existence." Fifteen similar centers have emerged around the continent in hopeful imitation of Esalen, which also runs many programs from a San Francisco office.

Named for an Indian tribe that long ago interrelated on the same 110 acres, Esalen is not, as some have thought, pronounced "East Salem." It should rhyme with wrestlin', one of the little spontaneities that sometimes erupt there. Elsewhere in the world and at other times in your life you prune, control and often conceal your feelings, but at Esalen you cultivate and flaunt them. You're not only permitted but urged to touch, hug and shout at people—or, if it should suit you, to stare them down. What you don't do is talk about how many miles you get to the gallon or where your children go to camp. There are really just two rules: don't be phony and don't, to use the vernacular of the hour, be uptight.

The Human Potential Movement has many outposts less boldly eclectic than Esalen and many leaders more conventional than Murphy. It is in fact so perplexingly amorphous that some of its own enthusiasts are hard put to define its boundaries. A thing of many overlapping sects and synods, it springs from the teachings of, among numerous others, Abraham Maslow, Carl Rogers, Paul Tillich, Erich Fromm, Teilhard de Chardin and the Zen Buddhists. It owes much to Aldous Huxley's idea that man is a "multiple amphibian" obliged to live at once in many contradictory worlds— biological, spiritual, emotional, cerebral, social—but guilty (after several centuries' obsession with technology) of neglecting most of these worlds to the point of atrophy. Our trouble, the movement's disciples preach, is that we are too much "cognitive" and too little aware of the "affective domain"—we think too much and only warily trust our senses. We ought to quit weaving tangled webs of polite, diplomatic but corrosive dishonesty and rely more on our untapped reserves of decency and strength. We should consider supplanting the notion of original sin with a new idea: original virtue. We should seize the unprecedented chance to control our social and psychological environment—or it will control us instead.

The movement is not only a mystique but a business, and a thriving one at that. Its most salable commodity is the "intensive group experience," known in some quarters as the "encounter" and in others as the "T-group" (T for training), or sensitivity-training workshop or training laboratory. T-groups often tend to deal with interpersonal and intergroup relationships rather than with the individual psyche, and have been adapted for use by corporations and other matter-of-fact organizations. The basic technique was first developed 21 years ago at the National Training Laboratories, a private organization. N.T.L. Institute for Applied Behavioral Science, in Washington, D.C., has its summer headquarters in Bethel, Maine and a network of hundreds of members around the country who profitably teach interrelating to all kinds of people sent off by their organizations: supermarket executives, admirals, stewardesses, teachers, dental students, policemen and even nuns.

One such concern—recently bought outright by Bell & Howell—is the Human Development Institute of Atlanta. H.D.I. offers not only the usual line of seminars and workshops but such ingenious, if somewhat Orwellian, products as an Interpersonal Relationship Kit and a 10-session series of tape-recorded instructions on getting along called Encountertapes.

It's too bad something as juicy as this phenomenon can't have a catchier title than the Human Potential Movement, but dialects vary widely from one outpost to another, and it's a wonder there's any single phrase acceptable to so mixed a lot of pitches and personalities. Awash in a glossary siphoned half from the hippies and half from the social scientists, the movement makes for sobering eavesdropping. "You and I have got to have a dyad," somebody might say, referring to what used to be called a talk or a tête-à-tête. "I've got to work through this gut feeling I have about you and find out where I'm *at*." Soon afterward someone else might announce, "Well, that's the end of the lecturette—I just wanted to give you an overview about input before we got into feedback." (Sometimes, though one surely isn't meant to, one longs for some good, old-fashioned, phony, uptight New York cocktail banter.)

Many in the movement say there's a bit of the therapist in all of us—that we are vastly more able to help and confide in each other than we might think. The chief source of this idea is the Western Behavioral Sciences Institute in La Jolla, Calif., whose aim, its director Richard Farson says, is "not to redesign society but to help find ways for society to design itself." W.B.S.I.'s most prestigious staff member is Dr. Carl Rogers, who spent the first half of his career developing the "client-centered" school of psychotherapy. Since then he has been busy championing basic encounter groups.

The movement's other chief patron is Dr. Abraham Maslow, who teaches at Brandeis University and presides this year over the American Psychological Association. Maslow, who to Esalen's delight has called it "potentially the most important educational institution in the world," thinks science should study values, should address itself to the nature of love, honor, delight and trust, and that we should learn to evoke "higher order behavior" so that more of us can become what he calls "self-actualizing personalities" capable of having "peak experiences."

"We're skating on thin ice," Maslow says, "but at the same time we're coming up with ideas that should keep mankind busy for a century." He even talks of "taking religion back from the priests—or turning them into social scientists." Many of his colleagues think this has happened already. People often emerge from encounter groups virtually shouting, "I'm changed! I'm saved!" This feeling differs from religious conversion,

Carl Rogers says, "in that the person brings it about in himself, instead of getting it from the outside. It has more durability. This is really something new in social history."

Esalen sometimes is like a religious retreat, sometimes a Southern revival meeting, sometimes a Dionysian revel. You might be invited to learn meditation, seated for up to 40 minutes in your interpretation of the Full Lotus position, in quest of what is variously described as the White Light, the Black Void and the Blue Line. You might spend an evening pounding bongo drums.

You might see a divorced couple shriek their repressed grievances at each other until the cords on their necks stand out in taut relief. You might see a man throw another man out of a window. You might be asked to feel the faces of a roomful of strangers, or to "say hello and goodby with your hands" or to "make hostile animal noises" or to fast. You might see a lad emerge from a session radiant as a bride "because I finally worked through my hang-up about authority figures."

For $11 you can have an Esalen massage—"a special series of brush strokes," says its inventor, Bernie Gunther, a body awareness expert, "designed to cover the whole canvas of the body." One of the masseurs is an ex-junkie named Seymour, who has a magnificent biblical beard, comes from Opportunity, Wash., knows how to eat fire and bake bread, and who memorably told me during my massage that "your fingers should feel like hot fudge."

Massages last at least an hour and are given in the bathhouse, whose more conspicuous attraction is four giant tubs filled with water from hot sulphur springs. Each tub can hold up to 15 soakers, only sometimes segregated as to gender. The idea of nude coeducational bathing provokes a good many winks, nudges and leers—more in the uptight world outside than on the grounds. Some of the time, anyway, the attention of the bathers is fixed less on each other than on the mesmerizing open view of the Pacific. "The baths here are sort of holy," said an Esalen resident fellow, "but the kitchen is even holier." The first thing you get on arrival is a meal ticket, punched thrice daily. It reminds you vividly of schools and camps and childhood.

Feeling childlike is part of the whole Human Potential game. Max Birnbaum, who runs Boston University's Human Relations Laboratory in New York, says that in any effective group "people may regress toward adolescent behavior." At Esalen they do more: they go back to infancy. Not only do people publicly neck and nuzzle like teen-agers, but they sit on each other's laps like babies. And they cry a lot. Crying is a sort of status symbol—a necessary stopover on the path from emotional rigidity to joy. The idea seems to be, "I hurt, therefore I am." Richard Farson defends this: "We wade into the tears and through them," he says. "Tears usually accompany something pretty good. I like to be with a person when he's discovering something about himself—when he's yielding to his emotions and is spontaneous."

My first public tears fell during a session called a "microlab" early in my five-day encounter workshop. Thirty of us were gathered in a room to do the bidding of Dr. William Schutz, an Esalen resident, who wrote the recent book *Joy: Expanding Human Awareness* (Grove Press) and who is one of the most gifted, adventurous and controversial group leaders in the country. Schutz had us split into subgroups of five people each, then decide which two in each group knew each other least. In my group these two turned out to be Steve, a handsome if inscrutable young man with a Tom Sawyerish lock of blond hair hanging in his face, and me. Steve and I were instructed to stand in diagonally opposite corners of the room and advance slowly toward each other. When we met in the middle we were to do whatever we liked to express our feelings about each other, just so it was nonverbal.

Well, I figured, Steve was certainly attractive, but I wasn't going to give him what I'd already heard described, derisively, as the "all-purpose cop-out Esalen hug" with which people known as "glib touchers" or, worse, "sensual pedants" were wont to greet the world at large. (Besides, I was much too eastern and uptight.) Instead, I'd pat him on the cheek—friendly, a bit California, yet dignified—smile pleasantly, and then move on.

Only that wasn't the way it worked out. Like tangoing, encountering takes two. When Steve and I met, he suddenly and quite forcefully shoved me back to the corner I'd come from. He seemed as surprised as I was and a trifle ashamed. I pretended with mock cheer that it didn't matter. "Well," I said as I resumed my place in the group, "I guess I ought to be afraid of *you*." I attempted a smile. "What are you smiling for?" Steve asked. "Do you think it's funny?" As a matter of fact, I didn't think so at all. In fact, I couldn't recall ever having felt so utterly, ludicrously rejected. Besides, as a girl named Pamela observed, my chin was atremble and aquiver, so why didn't I just go ahead and cry? Well, I did, in unlovely sobs that must have looked like sideways figure eights. Crying made me feel better and the others like me better, because I was exposing and expressing my real feelings. I was being authentic and congruent and living in the Here-and-Now. It was a rare and heady feeling.

Esalen also is interested in the There-and-Then. There's a good deal of talk about "trips," not via airlines or drugs but with fantasy, in a technique known as the "guided daydream." People are frequently found lying on mattresses, or just sitting on chairs with closed eyes, going back into their childhoods, or into dream worlds. Many of these journeys are led by Esalen's resident eminence Dr. Frederick Perls, the founder of a psychological approach called Gestalt therapy. Perls, a bearded chainsmoker of 74 who wears berets and parachute jumpsuits, provides Esalen with more than just a dollop of the atmosphere—or at least the accent —of old Vienna. He holds "dream workshops" in which group members act out every small aspect of their dreams or fantasies. If you dreamed your aunt was having a hot dog at the luncheonette, you *be* your aunt, *be* the hot dog, *be* the luncheonette. Eventually, in so doing, you will arrive at whatever impasse is troubling your emotional life, and if all goes well you will integrate the fragmented and seemingly unrelated aspects of your personality. These sessions can be extremely dramatic. In one I saw a young man who had at first seemed very pompous and inhibited decide, to the robust cheering of a group whom he had earlier bored, "I'M NOT CRIPPLED! I'M NOT DEAD!"

On one trip guided by Schutz, a divorcee recreated in fantasy her entire life, beginning with her own emergence from her mother's womb. She wept for a puppy whose death in her childhood she had never mourned, and went on—her voice gradually changing from newborn infant's squall to a little girl's treble to its present alto pitch—to the birth of her own children. In another session a man complained of an inordinate fear of death. He was 26, the same age at which his father died. He was thereupon made to "die" in fantasy, be "buried" and "reborn" while his group, by the spooky light of one candle, kept humming "OM."

I had a fantasy trip too. Bill Schutz led it. He told me to take off my glasses, lie down on a mattress and shut my eyes as the group drew near around me. I was to picture myself being very, very tiny and entering my body any way I chose. I went in by the mouth, clam-

bering over giant white teeth which despite their gold
inlays resembled the rocks down where the Esalen land
meets the Pacific. I slid down my slippery and rather
claustrophobic throat and into the torso. It was a long
and vivid journey that lasted an hour or so, with
stops at a sunny beach on Cape Cod, in a room lined
with paisleyish red and yellow watered silk like the end
papers of old books, a zoo whose cage bars were in fact
my ribs, a secret sliding rock panel behind my lungs
that led down to the intestines. I had a ride on a roller
coaster that led out of my body, and went back in, the
second time via the eyes, which inside were like little
rooms with railings on all the walls. I went back to the
beach again, where there was a nice group of strangers
whose names, it was quite clear, were Robin, George,
Sally and a baby named Kitty. They offered me some
of their picnic lunch and invited me to join them for a
walk, which I did with pleasure.

That walk led to a room with sticky red walls. As
I described this room Schutz gently said, ''There's a
calendar on that wall there—can you tell me what the
date on it is?'' Sure I could: the date was April 1948,
which was when I was in eighth grade and probably
liked myself less than at any other time in my life.
There followed a vignette about playing a loathsome
game called German dodgeball in the girls' gymnasium
of Skokie Junior High School, the entire floor plan of
which I was suddenly able to recall in precise, Nabo-
kovian detail. I wished aloud that I'd got an excuse
from the school nurse from this gym period, because
I had to wear an ugly leather-and-wire mask as a
glasses guard and I was self-conscious enough as it was.
Then, for some reason, came a side trip down to
my feet (which I had always, especially in eighth grade,
considered much too big but which now seemed just
right), and another detour to hands and fingers. From
this territory, I reported with delight, it was possible

to return not by a laborious climb but in a handy elevator that zoomed me nonstop back up to the shoulder.

The upshot of all this, Schutz later explained, was that I was in effect reborn, exorcised of my unflattering self-image as an awkward 13-year-old. I'd thought this was a ghost I had laid long ago, but apparently not, because exposing it in this public fantasy caused me to understand as nothing ever had before the meaning of words like *satori* and *nirvana*. For the first time since I got to Esalen people told me I didn't look uptight at all.

Now and then somebody leaves the premises feeling a little *too* euphoric. They tell at Esalen of the girl who was so ecstatically turned on by her encounter group experience that, while she was waiting to go home at the San Jose bus station, she ran up to hug and kiss everybody else waiting there and had to be carted away to an institution. Such incidents, known in the trade as "psychotic breaks," happen only a tiny percentage of the time. The rationalization is that if you crack up at Esalen, or at some other encampment of the movement, you probably would have done the same thing somewhere else—perhaps somewhere less "supportive." Still, that such things occur at all raises questions about the ethics of tampering with people's unconscious minds, and gives pause to the movement's leaders as well as ammunition to its enemies.

These enemies, if they were to congregate in one room somewhere, would have little in common but their misgivings, which vary spectacularly in nature and validity, and could be phrased more or less as follows:

(1) *The movement may be medically irresponsible.* When I described my "guided daydream" to Dr. Milton Kline, a New York psychiatrist who specializes in hypnotherapy, he said it sounded to him exactly like

hypnosis which is "a very intense behavioral experience which at times may have some contraindications" and questioned the advisability of "breaking down ego defenses unless the patient has been reasonably well-evaluated."

(2) *The movement is anti-intellectual.* When a schoolteacher in an Atlanta T-group protested, "I think this is a lot of weird crap!", he was automatically reprimanded. "Don't say think, say *feel.*"

This priority of gut over brain strikes some critics as decadent and dehumanizing. Dr. Silvano Arieti, another New York psychiatrist, warns that "if we escape from cognitive processes we return to a prehuman state. Only the most primitive of emotions do not need a cognitive counterpart. It is only with full understanding that we can get to the emotional core of things." Abraham Maslow himself cautions that some elements of the movement do "hover on the edge of anti-intellectualism." George Steiner, a writer and Cambridge University professor who gave an Esalen weekend seminar this winter, later asked, "What's the point of self-discovery if there's nothing, or very little, there to discover? All that's accomplished by having them go even deeper inside themselves is to show them what bores they are."

(3) *The movement is a hotbed of Communists or, anyway, anarchists.* More to the point, the movement is strongest in California, which is among other things a hotbed of suspicion. Murphy says Esalen has been attacked by John Birchers, "bugged" and much investigated. But such attentions have never resulted in any real charges.

(4) *The movement is led by dope fiends.* This is entirely wrong; the movement's whole point is to turn on without drugs.

(5) *The feelings the movement induces frequently don't last and can't be transplanted in the soil of real*

life. But Dr. Farson replies, "Do we expect sunsets to last, or a symphony? Isn't it too much of a burden on the experience to ask it to go on indefinitely?"

(6) *The movement can breed narcissism.* Well, it does nothing to discourage some 22-year-olds from thinking that their life histories contain the most fascinating subject matter in all Western civilization. Dr. Chris Argyris, who is a Yale professor and a T-group authority, feels, however, that this is true only of some elements within the movement when "the learning process encourages the experiencing of feelings [any old feelings] as an end in itself."

(7) *The movement breeds a kind of "emotional elitism."* When I took my shoes off once in California I was asked, "What would the people in your office think if they could see you *now?*", as if nowhere else on earth did people ever go barefoot, admire trees or stop to pick up pebbles. A lady devotee of the movement at a party in New York announced, "I'm the *only* person here who can actually *feel*."

(8) *The movement legitimizes and fosters promiscuity.* This charge is leveled mostly at Esalen, where there seems to be a lot of bedding down with new-found friends—or at least a lot of talking about it. Encounter groups discuss the nuances of people's sex lives with far more frankness and in far more detail than is customary elsewhere. Carl Rogers thinks that the "whole concept of groups getting emotionally quite close *is* very threatening to many people and *can* raise the prospect of sexual contact." But Esalen, its friends point out, didn't invent the sexual revolution, nor did the movement in general. Perhaps the candid discussion of sexual and marital problems does some good. Rogers thinks highly of "couples workshops" in which, he says, "we've saved a lot of marriages—some of them before they ever took place."

(9) *The movement constitutes a massive invasion*

of privacy. It does, in fact, sometimes seem a jumbo game not of "I've Got a Secret" but "I Had a Secret, and Here's What It Was." To quote Steiner again: "Making it a social goal and a moral obligation for people to advertise themselves—embarrassing them into telling publicly about privacies of the body and the psyche—is a form of tyranny."

(10) *The groups could be used for brainwashing.* Murphy admits "groups are generally benign but sometimes get mean." Dr. Argyris, however, doesn't worry. The objectives of such groups, he says, "are to help an individual learn to be able to reject that which he deeply believes is inimical to his self-esteem and to his growth—and this would include, if necessary, the rejection of the laboratory [or encounter group] experience."

(11) *The movement's concerns are trivial and irrelevant to the desperate problems of the day.* Many people object that they'd rather talk about Vietnam or assassinations than whether George is really jealous of Edith. Some branches of the movement, however, are rigorously concerned with social issues. Esalen is one of several organizations that have become involved in workshops in which police forces are confronted by residents of their cities' ghettos. In a recent New York seminar, I saw a black-power advocate enlighten (and scare) a roomful of city housing-project managers, some of whom confessed they weren't even sure who Malcolm X was. They departed, it is hoped, somewhat better equipped to cope with racial incidents that may develop this summer.

It is tempting to speculate what might happen if these confrontations occurred on a wider, higher scale. What if more places emulated marathons Esalen has held in San Francisco, catalogued as "Interracial Confrontation as a Transcendental Experience"? What if Carl Rogers were taken up on his offer to allow mem-

bers of his staff to lead a mass black-white encounter
in Watts? What if the Paris negotiations with North
Vietnam were suddenly to proceed under terms of absolute candor? What if James Earl Ray and Sirhan
Bishara Sirhan had been exposed to this rare amalgam
of forthrightness and trust?

Maybe people like them are being reached now.
W.B.S.I. has an $80,000-a-year foundation grant to
apply the basic encounter technique in a whole school
system—everybody, teachers, pupils and administrators, involved in the eight high schools, 50 elementary
schools and one college run by the Immaculate Heart
of Mary order in Los Angeles. Esalen has a $21,000
grant for a project administered by Dr. George I.
Brown of the University of California at Santa Barbara
experimenting with sensitivity-training techniques in all
levels of elementary and high schools. Esalen also has
had liaison with, among others, the Peace Corps,
Stanford University and the Episcopal Diocese of California. This month it is holding an extended international seminar on "The Value of Psychotic Experience"
and in September it will experiment with new treatments
for schizophrenics at the Agnew State Hospital. Esalen
also has a resident fellowship program, which this year
drew a Jesuit priest, two landscape architects and 18
others. This may someday expand into a full-scale college.

Is this whole movement just a fad, destined to
fade from memory like Hadacol, the Twist, wheat germ,
the Holy Rollers and the Maharishi? Will we all sit
around in the 1990s reminiscing about the silly old
days of T-groups, body awareness and Interpersonal
Relationship Kits? Will all that remains be a few yellow-
ing Christmas cards from friends we met in encounter
groups?

The prognosis is more hopeful. Michael Murphy
himself concedes that of the 150 approaches Esalen

has so far identified as means of expanding the human potential, some will indeed pass away unlamented. But "if we don't experiment with them," he says, "how will we know which are the good ones?" Some of them, in fact, are good. Some might vastly expand our capacities to learn, to love, to feel deeply and to create. Some might make our lives less fragmented and staccato and more reflective. Some might help us live less in the subjunctive tense than in the present. Some might make our thoughts more peaceful, our families and friendships more direct, our organizations of all kinds more harmonious. Some might improve the world, and the world wants improving.

SENSITIVITY TRAINING: BOON OR MENACE?

BY DONNA GILL

Sensitivity training.

This is a term that is misunderstood, hard to define, hailed as the savior of education by some, thwarted as a so-called brainwashing technique by others, and generally controversial.

It's been around for a few years now, in one form or other, but it stirred widespread interest in Chicago only this week. Sensitivity training sessions were held in private homes and directed by a teacher from Evanston Township High school, though not sponsored by the school. People wrote and called THE TRIBUNE to seek information on sensitivity training itself.

The techniques of such training vary. There is no one set pattern, and much of it depends on the "trainer" himself. It can vary from discussion groups or self-criticizing and group-criticizing sessions, where the mood itself varies from talk to heated argument, to more than 100 games to be played.

Donna Gill is a staff writer for the Chicago Tribune.

"Sensitivity Training: Boon or Menace?" first appeared in the Chicago Tribune *(January 26, 1969) and is reprinted here courtesy of the* Chicago Tribune.

The games themselves have many aspects: passing an orange around a circle, chanting arm in arm,
crawling around and touching each other as you are
wrapped in sheets or blankets, swimming nude in
groups, bathing together, mimicry, and just staring eye
to eye with another person.

At its best, its supporters say, sensitivity training
is a form of group experience that will make the individual lose his hangups and become innovative, more
of an individual, loving, more aware of himself and his
true feelings, more sensitive of the feelings of others,
and more creative.

At its worst, its detractors say, sensitivity training
becomes a form of group pressure and brainwashing
that makes the subjects accept the lowest common denominator in morals, be vulnerable to anti-church and
anti-family beliefs, destroys individuality, could lead to
sexual promiscuity, creates neurotics, and reduces people to vegetables unable to do anything but accept the
group's orders.

There are also those who take a middle view.
They say sensitivity training is good—if handled by a
competent professional, preferably a psychiatrist, and
if the persons involved are suited to such sessions and
have no deep problems.

"If someone feels very alienated, out of touch with
other people, feels remote, and you put him in a group
whose members are ploying each other, he may move
away even more and become completely autistic," said
Dr. Jules Masserman, co-chairman of the Northwestern
university psychiatry department.

"If you have someone already fairly well-bal-
anced, and he feels he wants to explore other horizons
and knows where the limits are and how to keep his
maturity and sanity in limits, then it's fine," he said.

"But you have to individualize it, and it takes a
great deal of experience and training on the part of the

leader. A swimming teacher knows you don't throw the whole class into the pool at once because someone might not know how to swim and might drown or get hurt."

The danger of such sessions in the elementary or high schools, he said, is that "you cannot generalize on any of it and a great many of these teachers just are not trained. You cannot take just a general class of teen-agers who have all sorts of individual characteristics and just willy-nilly subject the class to any one procedure."

Whatever the dangers or procedures or good points, sensitivity training has a foot-lock on the country and is used, in one form or another, in business or management training, in churches, youth groups, and schools. It is in great use in California.

For part of its research, THE TRIBUNE contacted two professors at Chicago Theological seminary. Both have worked extensively in group therapy sessions.

Dr. Arthur Foster, a professor of theology and personality, admitted that parents upset by the sessions involving their children were not unusual.

While some of the Evanston parents said the sessions helped their children, most complained that after the sessions their children were rebellious, engaged in shouting sessions, woke up not knowing where they were, suffered mental set-backs, cried continuously, and were generally confused.

"In the process, sensitivity training is going to shake a lot of people up," Dr. Foster said. "If the parents feel that way about the training, they ought to be in a T-group [training group] with their kids. The answer to the generation gap is to get together. That type of response on rebellion is inaccurate. It won't give rebellion, but it might bring it out in the open. The kids are in a much clearer position on this than their parents."

The parents did not think so. And throughout the country, small and large groups of parents and other groups are springing up to do battle against an activity they say is ruining their children.

Dr. Foster said sensitivity training is a loosely-used term that also includes forms of group dynamics: T-group training, auto-criticism, human relations training, Synanon Games clubs, basic encounter groups, self-honesty session, self-examination, and human potential workshop. Much of the trend originated in the National Training laboratories in Bethel, Maine.

"It is a study in the processes of change and the dynamics of planned change in society," he said. "It studies the dynamics of change in society, and what it takes to maintain a group, a society, or an institution, while at the same time bringing about change, or innovation."

He believes it will lead to good changes in education. He also believes it will lead to changes in people.

The critics believe the changes will mean that the person is open to the type of brainwashing used by the North Koreans on American prisoners of war during the Korean conflict.

Dr. Foster said the technique pretty well strips a person to the core, which is a common denominator of both brainwashing and sensitivity training.

He said that then, when the person is rather emotionally-stripped, if you were to brainwash him, you would apply coercion and threat.

But in sensitivity training, you rebuild and help the individual see himself as such. He said it is a matter of motive. Many of the groups who wrote THE TRIBUNE said that it is dangerous to get a person in such a vulnerable position at what they termed the "mercy of the leader."

Foster admitted there is possible danger, but said that something so "innovative and with such potential" should not be discontinued because of a fear of a possible abuse.

"I think it is the most innovative educational thing going on," he said. "I wouldn't indorse everything, but it's moving in a fresh kind of direction."

He said there is always a danger with an unqualified leader. He described some T-group sessions as taking about 12 persons and building a little society. He said it is always possible to come up with the demonic society the boys constructed in William Golding's "Lord of the Flies," but that the leader should be there "to see nothing is destroyed that shouldn't be."

"This little community could turn into a tyranny of group," he said. "It often happens in the process. At a certain moment, you get the whole group zeroing in on one person to try to make him think what they think. Then you get a wolf pack effect. Then it is time for the leader to zero in and get the group to see what they are doing to Joe. Since no leader is perfect, sometimes he doesn't pick up what's happening."

But, he said, he himself has not experienced it as a "dangerous thing." He said he could see much use of it to promote black-white understanding, for management to understand the role of labor, to increase church understanding and participating, and for couples.

His colleague, Dr. Ross Snyder, professor of religious education and pastoral psychology and a pioneer in group dynamics, did not always agree.

"There are great dangers that can be done by people who do not know what they are doing," he said. "You get things roused up that you might not have the knowledge to really cope with. You often end up with people who have learned a new way of being impersonal to each other.

"You've learned a new bag of tricks. You've learned new ways to be hostile and still appear to be friendly. For many, it just equipped them better to be hostile to each other and feel superior to those who had not had sensitivity training.

"Part of the problem is that people need to stay in the therapeutic group. All these very short term things may finally leave people more lonely than they were before they entered it."

He said one might learn how to manipulate other people, "but that's violating the rules." He also does not think sensitivity training should be done on teenagers.

"Potentially it could be very dangerous to teens," Dr. Snyder said. "It is clear that nobody, including the psychiatrists, knows how to work with teen-agers. With them, you should stick with communications skills and some of the basics of getting along with people. A teenager's identity is very fragile. You may tear him apart without knowing that you are. What they need is experience in being in places where they are treated as human beings.

"In some sessions, everybody will go after one person for what he's doing or not doing for the group. No holds are barred, in some forms. This is more than what most teen-agers can take."

Dr. Synder said sessions that lead to table thumping, shouting, and crying, need leaders "who know how to get contact back with these people."

But if it's done right, and with the right people, Dr. Snyder believes such sessions would "help people discover what their own feelings and attitudes are toward other people and what strategies they have used toward others."

But to Edgar C. Bundy, executive secretary of the Church League of America, Wheaton, "the main purpose appears to be the breakdown of all inhibitions, moral and physical, of the participants." He believes it is "turning some people into manipulated zombies."

The league's News & Views newsletter of October,

1968, attempted to describe some of the things done in sensitivity training and give its views on their merits.

It described nonverbal communications exercises in which people held hands for two hours without speaking and were instructed to allegedly "get really acquainted with your group. Let them realize that you are interested in them."

The newsletter went on to say that what followed was a "communal kissing mill." It described reports of other sessions with five men rocking a girl like a baby, men hugging each other, and people wrestling on the floor and slapping each other to awaken sensory awareness.

The newsletter writer admitted there is no traceable link among all groups practicing sensitivity training, but added the opinion that "this does not negate the historical fact that self-criticism is a step in the communist brainwashing technique.

But parents who wrote THE TRIBUNE were not talking about communistic influences. Some said they were concerned because a person had to "tell all" in such a session, and eventually told all the family troubles and gave others ammunition to use against them. Others said they believed that those controlling the sessions could thus control the minds and opinions of the children and mold them for a cause.